Notes from the
RAINFOREST

Photo by Susanne Lauten

Notes from the
RAINFOREST

George Faludy

ISBN 0-88882-104-2

Publisher: Anthony Hawke
Editor: John Robert Colombo
Designer: Gerard Williams
Composition: Accurate Typesetting Limited
Printer: Gagné Printing Ltd.

Publication was assisted by the Canada Council
and the Ontario Arts Council.

Hounslow Press
A Division of Anthony R. Hawke Limited
124 Parkview Avenue
Willowdale, Ontario, Canada
M2N 3Y5

Printed and bound in Canada

Front Cover Photo by Susanne Lauten

Acknowledgements

The pages that follow are the gleanings and expansions of notes taken by an inveterate scribbler during two months of semi-isolation in a small cottage on Vancouver Island in 1987. That the lucubrations of an elderly Hungarian poet should be of use to anyone in this country seems to me far from certain. Nevertheless, here they are.

I should like to express my thanks first of all to my friend E., *unico horum foliorum satori,* who took my barely decipherable Hungarian scrawls and gave them new life in English—to the point that the grateful author, checking over the results, has more than once been forced to the amused conclusion that he couldn't have said it better himself.

Throughout history poets, when they have eaten at all, have chewed the bread of patronage; and in this age, dominated as it is by Maritain's twin fallacies—"Money is prolific and the useful is the good"—there are no more patrons. Successive Canadian governments have, through the Canada Council and the Secretariat of State for Multiculturalism, filled me with grateful astonishment by their unfashionable assumption that poets are better employed wielding pencils than selling them on the street in tin cups. I wish to thank both organizations for having enabled me to devote an entire year, including the two-month period of which the following pages are a journal, to poetry.

George Faludy
Toronto, February, 1988

His necessities he purchased himself in the bazaar, and he prepared all his own food, using a spirit lamp to boil the water for his tea and coffee, as he told me that it was more economical than a fire. Doing without servants, he said, was a great source of peace, comfort and repose, and he certainly adopted Schopenhauer's ideas that the two great principles in life were to live, if possible, without pain and without ennui.

> F. F. Arbuthnot, "Life and Labours of Mr. Edward Rehatsek," Journal of the Royal Asiatic Society, July, 1892

May 27

For an Eastern European who has possessed five passports and been hounded from pillar to post for nearly eight decades, the most thrilling thing about flying from Toronto to Vancouver—more exciting really than the spectacle of the Rockies below—is to emerge from the airplane after four hours and find himself in the same huge, safe country; no passports, no *Kontrolle* (that sinister German word), no possibility of being sent back *there*. (You know where *there* is.)

Exiles sometimes appear rather ungrateful to the natives of hospitable countries, not really appreciative of their best qualities. What the natives don't know is that to the exile from certain countries the chief attraction of heaven itself would be the fact that it's not *there*.

*   *   *

From my bedroom window on a North Vancouver hillside, the city looks a bit like San Francisco, lights twinkling in the fog. In the afternoon it looked, to my eyes at least, better than San Francisco: the same undistinguished architecture, to be sure, but relaxed, unpretentious, and with no desperate chic in sight. In front of a department store I found a Tibetan monk begging with great dignity in his saffron robes. Almost any place else in the Western world he would be, I imagine, a local sight. In Vancouver (which an American poet once described to me as being "as laid back as a duck's ass") he was just a Tibetan monk in front of a department store. Canadian reserve, I decided long ago, is a more impressive quality than New York sophistication.

The architecture, though, is another matter. For all the other things it excels in, the Anglo-Saxon genius has never since the reign of Elizabeth I expressed itself in building. Even the best of it, Georgian, was stolen from an artist's sketchbook of Dalmatia. It's so bad, in fact, that everywhere from Melbourne to Los Angeles, from Chicago to Liverpool, blocks of new high-rises, hideous in themselves, come as a relief to the eye. It's no accident that the society that created the industrial revolution has also created the world's ugliest urban landscape to house its workers.

For anyone with his priorities in order, however, it is still a greater pleasure to stroll in Toronto, where in twenty years I have never encountered a serious public incivility, than in Paris, where you can't leave your doorstep without running into one.

May 29

Flashy billboards beside a B.C. highway: the car moves towards them like a donkey pursuing a carrot hanging from a stick. This, more than a "rat race," seems an apt image of life in the post-industrial, but still buck-chasing West.

May 30

O solitudo, sola beatitudo! Early morning mist, familiar Toronto-like sea gulls, a fog horn, a bumpy docking, embraces from friends and a long, long car ride—then I found myself alone in the cottage lent to me by the friend of a friend, a generous and trusting soul who has turned me loose without previous acquaintance in his two-room cottage. It is simply but comfortably furnished, has walls lined with books to the ceiling, and radiates, as houses sometimes do, the good sense, taste, and happiness of its owners. If I were fifty years younger I would have jumped for joy during my first inspection of the library, several times larger than my own and all well chosen. As it is, I unpacked toothbrush, clothes, and notebooks, poured myself a brandy, and went for a stroll in the neighbouring forest, an awe-inspiring piece of nature extending from here to the Arctic Circle, except for a stretch or two of water, and laughably known as "the bush."

After ten minutes' walking I was lost—seriously lost. Feeling the slightly sick sensation of incipient panic coming on, I sat down on a fallen tree and calmed myself by fanta-sizing improbably laudatory newspaper articles headed "Nobel Nominee Missing in B.C. Bush" and so on. I was still musing on this theme when a small dog bounded up, closely followed by a young man in a plaid shirt who kindly led me home—which turned out to be about a hundred yards away. After that the old fool poured himself another brandy and, for the past hour or so, has been sitting here at the writing table watching the darkness creep up as softly as a cat-burglar.

*   *   *

When I was young the interiors of little houses such as this one—surrounded by forest, loaded with books, warmed by a wood-burning kitchen stove—always filled me with envy and schemes for obtaining one of my own to complete my happiness. But loyalty to one's vocation, if it happens to be poetry, generally means foregoing such luxuries or enjoy-ing them merely as a temporary guest. The odd thing is, however, that although I love dachas as much as ever, the envy is gone. One of the best things about growing old (or even growing up, for that matter) is the way one gradually learns to contemplate things without coveting them: to treat "life as a vehicle for contemplation and contemplation as a vehicle for joy," as a Spanish philosopher once put it.

The curious thing about contemplation, in the real sense

4

of the word, is that it implies renunciation. A man looking at a woman with lust in his heart is not "contemplating" her any more than he could be said to be contemplating a painting in a gallery if his chief thoughts were of how to get his hands on it and take it home. Possession, as a little reflection shows, is an ephemeral joy, whether it be a question of real estate or of sex. Contemplation goes on forever.

*   *   *

"The beautiful is that which we desire without wishing to devour it. We desire that it should be."
—*Simone Weil*

June 1

Cool, light rain falling outside, slight scent of woodsmoke through the cottage as I burn a log in the stove. I keep thinking of this place as a rainforest, though Webster says that they are found only in the tropics. In any case it would be hard to imagine a more *limpid* wilderness than this, or one more beautifully clothed in moss and cold dew — it's like Brazil at the dawn of an ice age.

Other forests I have known: the Wienerwald, those well-groomed acres outside Vienna where people from Mozart to Mahler, Freud and Wittgenstein, have gone to repair the psychic damage of what is surely the world's most morbid city; the scruffy looking woods around Camp Atterbury, Indiana, where among six-foot snow drifts I once served in that bizarre and short-lived branch of the U.S. Army, the Habsburg Legion (the brainchild of FDR and Cordell Hull, who for a time entertained the mad notion of restoring the Austro-Hungarian Empire after World War II); the real rainforests of New Guinea, full of leeches, snakes, and the discarded pop bottles of the U.S. Army; and, finally, one of the last primaeval forests of Hungary, which, as a political prisoner, a walking skeleton in rags, I had to help cut down in the name of socialism. Those acres of massacred oak and cherry still come to mind whenever I hear anyone use the words "socialism" and "progress."

*   *   *

A note on Marxist *Kulchur*: Following Soviet usage, in Hungarian, surnames (which precede Christian names in that language) were for a while written only as initials, as for instance *Lenin. V. I.* Victor Hugo thus became *Hugo V.,* and on the 150th birthday of that poet many thousands of listeners wept with laughter when Radio Budapest announced: "Today we are celebrating the 150th anniversary of the birth of Hugo the Fifth."

Just to be fair I ought to mention that some months ago I heard a Toronto radio announcer hesitate briefly when announcing a future programme, then come out with "the flora and fauns of British Columbia".

*   *   *

When I first set eyes on English industrial cities it occurred to me that more than their poverty, perhaps, it was the unrelieved ugliness of their surroundings that crushed the spirits of 19th-century urban workers. This was something our Mediaeval ancestors, whose lives were even harder, seem to have understood instinctively. Today we gape with admiration looking at the remains of their towns. Is this really so hard to grasp? Among those breaking their heads over the appalling decay of American cities, is there no one who can see that the essential difference between the life of the slum dweller and the suburbanite is not so much quantitative as qualitative and aesthetic? Who but a Mother Teresa could feel and behave entirely like a human being in a dung heap like Detroit?

*   *   *

Came across a book I had not known existed, Solzhenitsyn's 1978 Harvard commencement address (published by

Harper and Row as *A World Split Apart*), and was so engrossed in it that I burned the toast three times in the non-
automatic toaster. I got as far as page 35, where, marvelling,
one reads: "A fact that cannot be disputed is the weakening
of human personality in the West while in the East it has
become firmer and stronger.... The complex and deadly
crush of life has produced stronger, deeper, and more interesting personalities than those generated by standardized
Western well-being."

Mulling for a while over this statement—which contains
a tiny kernel of truth—I reflected on the consumer madness of Hungary, Polish rock groups with names like "Electric Orgasm," Red Army soldiers murdering to acquire
Mickey Mouse wristwatches, the flesh market of Prague
where for a pair of genuine Levi's you can...and so on.

Eventually I started to laugh. I laughed so hard that I went
out onto the porch where my whoops startled the birds off
their branches. Later I remembered and confirmed Gore
Vidal's rude comment on Solzhenitsyn in *Views From a
Window*: "The Russians displayed uncharacteristic humour
in letting this nut come to our shores."

*   *   *

Whatever the depths of their personalities, ordinary Russians are often capable of extremes of behaviour that leave a
Western observer appalled and touched at the same time. I
remember the account, first-hand it was claimed, about an
incident in 1945 when the Red Army were driving the Nazis
out of Hungary. At the mausoleum which housed the lead
coffin of the country's first great classical poet, Daniel
Berzsenyi, a Soviet captain and his company stopped to
inquire who was buried in such a splendid tomb. Upon
being told, the captain announced that he would love to be
buried, when the time came, in a lead coffin. Before his unit
left the area the captain was killed in a collision between his
jeep and a larger vehicle. His men, simple Russian and
Central Asiatic peasants who were obviously fond of him,

forced open the coffin, tossed out Berzsenyi's bones, and replaced them with the body of their dead officer—who thus became one of the oddest footnotes in the history of Hungarian literature.

One also remembers an incident during the 1956 Revolution when Soviet tanks were blasting their way down a Budapest street, shooting into the ground floors of houses until the entire structure collapsed. In the midst of this carnage an aged woman, lost and confused, wandered into the street before the leading tank, which stopped. The turret opened and a Russian popped up looking concerned. "Hurry, *babushka*, hurry!" he urged her, waving her out of the line of fire. That done, the massacre resumed.

East Europe knows hundreds of such instances of Russians combining humanity with barbarism. Is this what Dostoyevsky, Berdiaev, and Solzhenitsyn have in mind when they extol the "divine mission of the Russian people to save the world by compassion"? One also knows of SS and Gestapo men who loved Mozart and wept over dead pets. Should we talk of some similar divine mission placed on the shoulders of the German people?

*   *   *

On highways all over Canada I have seen crumpled deer and flattened squirrels, rabbits, and skunks—but never, so far, a raccoon. Are raccoons more careful travellers through the night? I have seen their eyes and those of their children like reflectors beside the road, waiting, planning their dangerous expedition to the other side, like refugees hiding while the border guards pass by.

June 2

The British Columbia forest lies as silent under its moss as an Ontario forest under snow. Such sounds as there are present no argument to the ear: a bird, a droplet rolling off a

8

leaf into the nearby pond, a rustling of leaves as some tiny creature goes about its business. Then silence again, so dense that the world seems made of it.

If we were truly sane, truly whole creatures, we would never tolerate the noise we make in the world. One does not have to be a Luddite to find our machinery obscene: Just emerge from this miraculous realm of silence when a motorcycle happens to be roaring and farting its way down the road and watch the universe shatter. Even our own speech is rarely more than a noise to disrupt the general peace of things. As far as that goes, how many words have I ever written as worth hearing as the splash of a frog leaping from a lily pad? A few. Maybe.

*　　　*　　　*

Reading Seneca over tea and toast this afternoon: *Cui cum paupertate bene convenit, dives est.* He who lives on friendly terms with his own poverty is a rich man. This was the sort of age-old received wisdom my generation was brought up on, so obviously true as to seem trite. There was a time a few years ago when it looked as if a rebellious generation might be rediscovering it all for themselves, but that bubble has long since burst. Those kids in the '60s were rediscovering very little and rejecting even less. They didn't really turn their backs on the rubbish their parents had accumulated, they just hauled it off to the wilderness where they watched television in geodesic domes built of plastic and discarded car parts. In any case that's the version of the "greening" of America I once saw in California, and it was a dismal sight.

*　　　*　　　*

It is no accident that the German word *Spiessbürger*, like *Schadenfreude*, has no exact equivalent in any other European language, for both reach in the heart of Europe a pinnacle of perfection less frequently attained elsewhere. Of course they are by no means restricted to Central

Europe. *Schadenfreude* is universal, and I met a *Spiessbür-ger* in Vancouver just the other day, so typical a specimen that I am tempted to try to list the defining attributes of the species.

A *Spiessbürger* is a petit bourgeois who has achieved a level of philistinism remarkable enough for his neighbours to have noticed it. Though perhaps not wealthy himself, he values property above all things; given the chance, he will invariably idolize a Hitler, a Mussolini, a Pétain or a Pinochet; he will consider any prejudice he happens to share as an immutable law of nature—unless the State decrees otherwise, in which case he will run to conform; he never gives to beggars; he is often prone to racism ("the snobbery of the poor"); like all of us he has sometimes wept in the theatre or cinema, but would be amazed to learn that the same intensity of emotion could ever be expended on similar situations (or anything else) in daily life.

The *Spiessbürger* is as common as grass in much of Europe (including England and excepting the Balkans) but, in my experience, is rather rarer in North America. Which is perhaps why when I was cornered by one the other day the Canadians around me looked at once pained and amused, causing me to reflect, not for the first time, that despite Central European origins and years of abortive escape attempts, I have finally landed in a very satisfactory place.

*   *   *

Why does one have an instinctive certainty that St. Mary Magdalene was a better person than St. Paul, Chuang Tzu than Confucius, and Mother Teresa of Calcutta than, say, St. Theresa of Lisieux? Perhaps it has something to do with the rather overweening self-confidence and dogmatic certainty of the latter group. *"Les meilleurs hommes,"* as someone once said, *"sont toujours un peu indécis."* It is a good point to remember in debates on such things as capital punishment.

June 3

Opening this notebook every night I am tempted to write in English and so keep the Hungarian poetic process rigorously separated from these nocturnal afterthoughts and musings. But I learned long ago that it is dangerous to attempt anything weightier than a letter to a friend in any language one is not entirely at home in. Once, for example, I carefully wrote the first draft of an academic address in English and asked E. to correct it for me. A half hour or so later I found him shaking, with tears of mirth streaming down his face, over a passage in which I had described a certain French poet as "not only a distinguished purveyor of French letters, but almost the only male member among those still writing Sapphics in the style of Lesbos."

E. himself has a wonderful store of similar howlers from two years spent as a teenager in Tokyo, when the Japanese were struggling with the new language imposed by their American occupiers. From these I remember the following: a traffic sign at a dangerous crossroads which read: HAVE ACCIDENT HERE; a sign outside a Ginza shoestore: LADIES SHOES IDEAL FOR STREETWALKING; a tailor's advertisement: GENTLEMEN HAVE FITS UPSTAIRS; and, outside the Tokyo water-filtration plant: DIRTY WATER PUNISHMENT CENTER.

Menus around the world provide endless examples of the same sort. I remember an evening many years ago at the house of Princess Ruspoli in Tangier during which the British writer Gavin Maxwell told me about a Spanish bill-of-fare which offered BALLS, CATALAN STYLE.

*   *   *

Among the few books I have brought with me is *Crocodiles in the Bathtub and Other Perils* by my old friend George Jonas. Perusing these essays over tea and toast this morning, I smiled at his usual dry wit and almost clinical way of leaving his opponents pinned and squirming like specimens for labelling: *Homo sovieticus canadensis, Feminista ferox jonasi.*

Although it has frequently left me feeling a bit further to the right than is comfortable for an old Social Democrat, more often than not over the years I have agreed with the common-sense views that have made his name anathema to packs of left-lib trend-hounds, those who think that the obscene government in Pretoria is the most oppressive in Africa, that Fidel Castro is a great friend of humanity, that the best way to redress past injustices towards women, blacks, homosexuals, baby seals, and the unemployed is revenge. Indeed the only area in which he makes me really uneasy is that of economics, and it was not until this morning that I realized exactly why.

In his essay *Renting Asunder,* after arguing reasonably and plausibly against government interference in the market place, Jonas goes on to say: "I'm not suggesting that interference is never justified. It is, in times of emergency, such as war, earthquake, or pestilence. Essential goods, including clean drinking water, may have to be rationed at such times to save lives, and I have no sympathy for profiteers who traffic in a market distorted by catastrophe." "Emergency" is the key word here, and my view of what constitutes one is different.

Throughout history it has been such a hard and frequently impossible task for people to feed, clothe, and shelter themselves and their families that the sight of others dead in the street from hunger, exposure, or pestilence was not until well after the Middle Ages unusual enough to constitute an emergency. In the last two centuries that has changed, at least in our part of the world—where a day spent in circumstances like those of Calcutta would be a calamity of major proportions. *In the presence of plenty, any real and remediable human misery constitutes an emergency, and the neglect of it on grounds of naturalness or inevitability just won't do.*

Although it is arguably sheer greed that has brought the West its current and possibly temporary degree of prosperity, it is by no means clear that greed is a necessary cause of the wealth of nations. Some groups, from the mediaeval Cistercians to present-day Mennonites, have accumulated quite a lot of money without anything resembling covetousness in their hearts. And it is worth noting that the Seven Deadly Sins, of which greed is one, were by no means a Mediaeval superstition, but a psychologically shrewd list of some of the chief sources of human unhappiness. Of those seven Jonas pays particular attention to envy, which he considers "the dominant preoccupation of our times" (I myself would nominate greed for top place) and the driving force behind an increasingly institutionalized "lust for parity." Towards lust itself he displays the benign tolerance one expects of a man who knows the world and whose priorities are based on moral economy rather than moral superstition. That being the case, one is puzzled by his attitude towards greed, which he seems to consider not only unsinful but positively virtuous—except of course in emergencies.

Granting Situation Ethics the point that some actions take on a different moral colouring in different situations—if a surgeon cuts you open it's called surgery, if I do it it's murder—the chief point about moral philosophy's Seven Deadly Sins is that they are moral attitudes that remain wrong under *any* circumstances. But even if one is too modern to accept this ancient bit of wisdom, the question of what constitutes an emergency remains. I have read that one Canadian child in ten knows real and frequent hunger in this generally overweight society. When does the emergency begin? One in five? One in two?

Here, on either count, is the heart of my disagreement with my old friend (who as a man, by the way, is far more humane and generous than a strict adherence to his own philosophy could account for): Such moral sense as I have not only recognizes but is largely founded upon the guilt-inducing and frequently inconvenient fact that I *am* my brother's keeper, and that greed is, among other things, one of several ways of denying that fact. The factory owner who keeps his workers living in near-misery is in the same general moral category as the man who makes fat profits in time of war or other calamity—and in my rather extensive personal experience he usually turns out to *be* the same man. It is not a "lust for parity" that makes us as a species more nearly resemble preying mantises than the creatures we have it in us to be. It is fear and the offspring of fear: hatred and greed.

*   *   *

And now, with the subject of money uppermost in my mind, I must tackle two requests from the Guggenheim Foundation for appraisals of two young poets asking for fellowships. One would have thought there were native English-speakers around better able than I am to evaluate their work. Be that as it may, I rather like the poems of both and can praise them to the skies without a bad conscience. My inclination in these matters (not always obeyed) is in any case to praise, on the grounds that it's the self-proclaimed task of these organizations to give away their money to impecunious talent, so they might as well get on with it.

The accompanying brochure says the Guggenheim gave away $6,336,000 last year. There's always hope for a society in which the ants can be persuaded to feed the grasshoppers.

June 4

Although there is no denying the general poverty of poets, in countries where poetry has a large audience there are other rewards. I remember two instances of this.

Taxis were practically non-existent in the Budapest of 1956, and, faced with an hour-long walk home late one night after a party, I was amazed to find one parked under a street lamp in Buda; but less surprised when the driver, slouched in his seat and reading a book, refused to take me on the grounds that he was "busy." Peering in the window I glanced at the page he was reading. "Is it any good?" I asked. "First rate!" he replied. "I'm relieved to hear it." "Why?" he asked, puzzled. "Because I wrote it." I had to show him the name on my identity card, but got my ride home, a free ride despite my protests.

In the summer of the same year I was sitting in the Száz Éves restaurant one afternoon writing a poem. At a nearby table a young man was courting his girl friend in the rather Victorian fashion then usual in Hungary. I glanced up from time to time to look at the girl, who was very beautiful, and each time I did so she smiled back. Finally the youth took a book out of his briefcase and demanded her attention by reading a love poem. I looked up and exchanged another smile with the girl. "Can't you stop looking at that idiot long enough to listen to this fantastic poem!" the boy exploded. At this there was a loud laugh and I saw my old friend the journalist Fedor Agnes (the Baroness Wesselényi) peering around the corner of a nearby booth. I put a finger to my lips, silently pleading with her not to embarrass the boy by telling him that the idiot and the author of the poem were the same man. She kept silent, but the little story appeared in the papers the next day.

Recognition is lots of fun, but I doubt that it ever caused me to write better poems than I have written since in the comparative obscurity of exile.

*   *   *

Sometimes when mentioning the love most Hungarians have for poetry I have noticed scepticism on the faces of Canadian friends. There seems no way to convince Anglo-Saxons of the truth of this, though this morning I suddenly remembered a rather persuasive local instance of the phenomenon.

Some years ago, when a friend was driving me to Buffalo, we stopped at the house of a Hungarian farmer outside St. Catharines, Ontario. This hospitable man raised turkeys and in many ways lived a Hungarian rural life in a North American setting. He served us wine in the parlour opposite a large, 19th-century style oleograph of Dante waiting on the Lungarno in Florence and seeing Beatrice for the first time. A little at a loss for conversation, I mentioned the picture and said something about Beatrice "Portarini". Our host seemed embarrassed and corrected me: "Portinari, Mr. Faludy, Beatrice Portinari was her name." Looking shyly into his wine glass, he quoted some lines describing Beatrice written by Dante's Hungarian translator, Michael Babits.

There was so little inherently improbable about a Hungarian turkey farmer quoting Dante that, until today, I had entirely forgotten the incident. But I wonder if it could have occurred in a similar setting among people of any other nationality.

June 5

The first mail has arrived from Toronto, most notably a long letter from E., who is wandering around his beloved Yugoslavia, after which he will go to India. E.'s travels always cost in air fare almost all the money he can scrape together. How he meets the other expenses is something of a mystery, but he does. His letter, postmarked Zagreb, arrived open. In most of East Europe that would mean it had been censored; in Yugoslavia it just means the gum on the envelope didn't work. He writes:

> As soon as the train crossed the border and we cleared customs I was thrown out of first class, lacking *dinars* to pay the supplement, and found myself wedged in a second class compartment with a young couple returning from factory work in France, an elderly man getting drunk on *rakija*, a teenaged boy who was staring thoughtfully at the breast of a young and strik-

ing Gypsy girl nursing her baby. That the Gypsy girl (and the old woman who was probably her mother) should have been sitting in the compartment was rather odd in northern Yugoslavia, where people have inherited from the Austro-Hungarian Empire a certain amount of anti-Semitic and anti-Gypsy feeling. I had never before seen a Gypsy in a compartment north of Beograd.

Once they finished marvelling at how badly I speak Serbo-Croat, more *rakija* was produced and time went by in a haze of tobacco smoke, marked only by empty bottles, folk songs, jokes, imprecations against the government and, amidst general hilarity, an attempt on my part to read the palm of the younger gypsy.

"We all staggered out at Zagreb, temporary friendships ended in the frank Yugoslav way, and I sat awhile over coffee in the station restaurant under the huge photograph of Marshal Tito. From one point of view Zagreb station is the East Block in a nutshell: dirty, filled with rather shabby people looking exhausted, patrolled by militia men in grim pairs. From another point of view, that of affectionate familiarity, it's filled with people who know who they are and like it; who sip their coffee or beer with enormous gusto, grateful for the smaller pleasures of life; who in spite of living in a police state are apt to speak their minds with disconcerting frankness.

My chum K. was not on duty at the hotel desk, so after showering I strolled through dear old Zagreb in the twilight: scent of bougainvillea everywhere, red flags flying in the parks, sidewalk cafés doing an uproarious business. With two-thousand calories (at least) in the form of *rakija* inside me, it seemed best to go without dinner. Tomorrow, when K. inspects the eminently marketable goodies I've brought with me, I'll go book-hunting. It's so good to be back here one could weep for joy."

With the possible exceptions of Rebecca West and Marshal Tito, I doubt that anyone has ever loved Yugoslavia more than E., nor is this any longer a mystery to me. Some months ago when the unexpected possibility of a short trip to that country presented itself, I grabbed it. After a week of rummaging in library archives among stacks of yellowing magazines and newspapers for early works of mine, I got on local buses and wandered through deepest Bosnia-Herzegovina, bemused at finding myself once again in a country filled with red flags and hammers and sickles — and liking the place a lot. Sometimes it reminded me of rural Hungary, at other times it revealed itself as a quite different country, populated by one of the most handsome peoples on earth: tall, stern, rather dour, but willing, when there was something to smile about, to smile. They are utterly without pretensions, and talking with strangers without a common language leaves one not only unexhausted but exhilarated.

For all E. says about Croat dislike of Gypsies, I saw the opposite everywhere, even in predominately Croat towns. At an outdoor café in Trebinje, a shabbily dressed Gypsy boy of ten or so was begging his way from table to table, and nearly everyone gave him something. That child had a face of startling beauty—not so the old woman sitting on rags at a street corner in Mostar, but she too, as long as I watched, was given coins. It was obvious that no one scorned or despised them, and in this Yugoslavia has an advantage over our more prosperous societies, where in many minds human worth is imbecilely confused with solvency.

It must be admitted that there is nothing resembling the elaborate courtesy, the cultivated *Höflichkeit* of Central Europe in Yugoslavia. People are short on please and thank you. But if every again, as so often in my life, I find myself friendless and penniless in a strange country, pray God it's a place like Yugoslavia and not some plastic paradise where, so often, the treatment one receives is, to a nicety, commensurate with one's probable credit rating.

*　　*　　*

18

An unsigned postcard from Zagreb: "The clerk at the desk told me the latest political *plaisanterie*: Of all systems, which is the least compatible with Communism? Answer: the central nervous system."

*   *   *

In Serbo-Croat, as in Hungarian and (I believe) in Russian, to ask about a man "What is he worth?" is to inquire about his character. In English it inevitably refers to his bank account.

*   *   *

A remark overheard and recorded by the Jesuit theologian Martin D'Arcy in a London omnibus: "Well, don't take on so, dearie. Be a philosopher and don't think about it."

*   *   *

Overheard by G. Faludy standing near an elderly couple of bewildered Canadians beneath a twenty-four-hour clock at Toronto's airport: "I don't known," said the husband. "It must be one of those new metric clocks."

June 6

Out sitting on the moss beside the pond this morning, I watched shafts of light pour down through intertwining branches in that cathedral effect which nature creates in her Gothic mood. For awhile I also observed a frog slowly munching up a dragon fly with the innocence of a child eating ice cream:

> The ugly vulture eats the dead,
>   Guiltless of murder's taint.
> The heron swallows living fish
> And looks like an ascetic saint.
>
> — *Bhartrhari, translated by J. Brough*

Religions—all of which seem to have been created to cope with the inevitable answer to Schopenhauer's question as to whether life is better suited to pain or to pleasure—can perhaps be divided into two general categories. In the first, the usual one, there are religions like Buddhism (a metaphysic in search of a mode of worship) and Christianity (a mode of worship in search of a metaphysic). To judge from statistics, the world is getting tired of both, and perhaps the main reason is not, as usually assumed, competition from the so-called scientific point of view. These religions have the drawback of limiting vision and interpreting experience according to very restrictive rules: they discourage interest in nearly everything outside themselves. Devout adherents to them seldom give the impression of looking for the truth of anything, presumably because they already possess it.

But one can imagine another sort of religion, vaguer but less presumptuous, like Seneca's as described in his forty-first letter to Lucilius: awe before the numinous, gratitude towards life, and offerings to a god frankly admitted to be unknown. Some Anglicans of my acquaintance seem in a rather ambiguous way to be aiming at something like this. As one of them explained to me not long ago, "It doesn't really matter whether the Resurrection actually happened or not—it's the significance of the event that counts." (This left me wondering, though not for long, what the significance of a non-event might be.) Perhaps what I am aiming at here is merely what Kenneth Burke meant when he said, "A person has the right to worship God according to his or her own metaphor."

In any case, I was thinking along these woolly lines earlier this evening as the kettle was going on the boil, and I reflected, with a surge of gratitude, what a great gift it has been to live seventy-six years on this astonishing planet. But, *pace* St. Thomas, thirst does not presuppose the existence of water, nor does a sense of gratitude imply a divine gift-giver. Or does it? Sometimes one does feel like walking to the porch and pouring a small libation of wine beneath the moonlight. The impulse, I am convinced, is foolish; the gratitude not.

*   *   *

It was a piece of good fortune, especially for a budding poet, to have learned in one's youth that what does not exist requires no explanation. A metaphysician, I was told by a respected teacher at the age of sixteen or so, is one who debases the coinage of language, effacing the imprint in order to render it dateless and placeless. Shillings, marks, and francs all come to resemble one another, shiny tokens to which you can assign any value you like, for they no longer have any of their own. Hence Plato blindly peering into the clouds and pronouncing on The Good and so on— as if it, or indeed anything else, existed apart from its instances.

*   *   *

One of the small pleasures I most miss with the demise of classical learning is Latin wordplay. Among the thousands of examples on record I have long had two favourites, one 19th-century Hungarian, the other World War II German. *Si mortalis immortalis Simor talis.* If any man be immortal Simor is such. It was written by a schoolboy in honour of Cardinal Simor. *Labitur Dux, dabitur Lux.* The Leader has fallen, light is given! It was written by a German poet when, for a few hours one day in July 1944, it was thought Hitler had been assassinated.

*   *   *

There is an article in a Hungarian paper about the persecution of the Hungarian minority in Rumania. It's true — but one nation of East Europeans complaining about the inhumanity of another one is really a sight for the gods. One remembers how in 1944 the Hungarian police enthusiastically rounded up 400,000 Jews so that Colonel Eichmann could ship them in cattle cars to Auschwitz, while in the meantime the Budapest papers went on yapping about *Russian* barbarism.

*   *   *

Listening to the radio late at night on Vancouver Island, you can bring in stations hundreds, even thousands of miles away—but what you hear is no better than the schlock they play all over Europe nowadays. In a lecture once I briefly touched on the debasement of popular music in the past hundred years, and was afterwards rather angrily contradicted by a young academic who insisted that the situation now was the same as it had always been, and those who didn't like it were "elitists."

The situation is not the same. Throughout the history of our civilization, there have been popular cultures, sometimes of a very high order—as demonstrated by early Greek oral poetry and the folk music of Russia and Rumania, among much else. One of the invaluable functions of these popular cultures was to form the basis of and nourish what for lack of a better term is called "higher culture".

Since the industrial revolution, however, something new has happened, and herein lies, I think the error of my young opponent. What happened was the increasingly rapid destruction of folk cultures everywhere, and with them the potential basis of any living higher culture. Is the music one hears everywhere today on the same level with, say, the Hungarian, German, or Spanish folk music that was played a century ago? Obviously not, for that formerly "popular" music is now popularly though of as "serious" or even "classical" music.

What intervened was the creation of the proletariat, a class of people whose ancestors made verse, music, and a variety of beautiful objects (including architectural objects) but who have themselves become utterly incapable of the same sort of creation. Nor is it elitist to point this out: no one who has roots in a living tradition—be he an Oxbridge scholar, a Transylvanian shepherd, or (if any still exist) an Appalachian balladeer—is going to mistake these howls over the air waves and in the discos of the West for anything but what they are: the mindless auto-eroticism of people who have been deprived by urbanization, mass media, and spiritual uprootedness of their entire cultural inheritance. Pop is the folk music of the proletariat—or would be, if the proletariat wrote it. For the rest, the charge of elitism is refuted by the fact that nowadays the taste of the so-called elite is generally just as impoverished as that of the people who work in their factories.

It is to the eternal credit of Karl Marx that he spent his life trying to figure out how to raise the industrial proletariat out of its misery; but this will not be enough to prevent him from remaining a laughing-stock of history for having insisted that those robbed of their spiritual heritage are thereby rendered somehow wiser than their ancestors and so fit to lead the rest of mankind, along with themselves, into paradise.

The proletarian is not defined by the way he makes his living, the level of his income, or the surroundings he lives in. A Mediaeval beggar was not a proletarian, nor is a Sicilian fisherman. The proletarian is a man or woman or child who has been robbed by fate of a rich inheritance and has learned to be content with the dregs of a debased, mass-produced culture, whether he lives in a slum or (as frequently happens) in the White House. To say that he ought to be abolished as a class is no more elitism than is saying that the naked should be clothed and the hungry fed—it's simply compassionate concern.

*   *   *

"It is not *badness*, it is the absence of *goodness*, which, in Art as in Life, is so depressing."

— *Freya Stark*

June 7

Not only people suffer under totalitarian regimes, but languages as well. The fates of the German and Russian languages under Hitler and Stalin have been documented. As far as I know, no one has yet undertaken to study the vulgarization and devalourization of Hungarian since World War II. Of course it is not only tyrants who kill languages: It is said that Japanese is becoming a kind of oriental Newspeak under the impact of pop culture and total industrialization, and the fate of English both as an international *lingua franca* and the bafflegab of Washington press conferences is notorious.

All this being the case, to find in one's hands a recent Russian novel in which the resources of the language are not only intact, apparently, but actually extended, is a miracle to be greeted with awe and gratitude. The book in question is *School for Fools* (*Shkola za durakov*) by Sasha Sokolov and translated by Carl Proffer.

Sokolov was born in Ottawa thirty-odd years ago, the son of a KGB man attached to the Soviet Embassay. Back home in the USSR he eventually had enough and, after a noisy and public hunger strike, was allowed to leave. A Canadian citizen now, he has also written another novel, but *School for Fools* must have been around some time in manuscript, for the publisher (Ardis) has used Vladimir Nabokov's comment—"infinitely touching"—as a jacket blurb. The comment is an understatement.

School for Fools, a not very long novel, is narrated by the twin personalities of a teen-aged Russian boy suffering from a form of schizophrenia too charming to be possible, but made plausible for all that by the author. It is a sustained reverie, a dialogue between the boy's two selves in midsummer at a dacha colony beside a lake. It is loaded with the Turgenevian scent of Russian summer, resin and heliotrope. With a stroke of the pen, as it were, it revives a literary culture long smothered in agitprop, diesel fumes, and Soviet vulgarity. There is little action in the book, merely a refraction of existence through the gentle eyes of a victim who is altogether more human than those around him. It is not your average page-turner, but is, I suspect, a masterpiece.

Has anybody in Canada heard of Sokolov? I had not, nor is it surprising. Mere literary merit is no more likely to get a book published in North America than in the USSR, albeit for different reasons. The works of such exiles as Aksenev, Limonov, and Solzhenitsyn are rushed into print for quite other reasons.

The praise on the jacket by well-known Russian writers—Nina Berberova, among others—is uniformly high, even ecstatic. Fairly ecstatic myself, and living in the same country as this remarkable man, I made inquiries. Jacqueline d'Amboise, once an officer with the Canada Council, informed me that the Council decided it could not help Sokolov because it had no jury which could judge Russian prose. Reasonable enough, but I wonder if any of them realized what slipped through their fingers that time.

Are you out there, Sasha? Don't despair. Nowadays dissident Russian hacks are regularly invited to the White House for lunch, but a greater fate than that awaits you sooner or later. Wherever you are and whatever you're doing to keep body and soul together, be sure that you are, hands down, the best writer of Russian prose anyone's seen in a long time. Feed quietly on that fact. You'll find it sustaining.

*   *   *

Madame K., who has moved to the south of Spain after some forty years of living in Tangier, has written me a rather sour letter:

> ...it hit me one day in a Malaga bookshop that in this motherland of Torquemada, the Inquisition, and *autos-da fé* there is not much anti-semitism nowadays. It would be interesting to know how this came about. Possibly because the Church, like more or less everything else except the tourist industry, is largely defunct.
>
> "There is a great absence of things to read. The modern Spanish imagination seems to have risen and

fallen in the persons of Picasso, Miró and Dalí. Of literature there is next to nothing, the bookshops offering translations or in desperation importing lust-along-the-Amazon novels. Here, as in Buenos Aires, Borges is assumed because of his vast auto-didacticism to be a Master. It could only happen in the Spanish-speaking world that an author is celebrated not because he can write, but because he can *read*.

*   *   *

On a more gentle note, E. writes this from Zagreb:

> I was strolling along the Ilica this morning (the street that most resembles Budapest) and saw on the other side a boy of perhaps eleven, very thin, tidily dressed, playing an accordion with his cap lying open on the pavement at his feet. The economy here is a shambles and one sees, apart from Gypsies, quite a few old women forced to beg because of inadequate pensions (about seventy-five dollars U.S. just now). But the sight of this child filled people with visible distress. A militia man walked past scowling at the pavement. Near me a woman stood at the curb with tears running down her face. (To add to the general effect, she was carrying a large volume of Gorky in her hand.) The whole scene might have been labelled *The Failure of Socialism*. There was no failure of humanity, however. The kid was taking in a fair amount of money. The wealth of this country is great, but intangible.

*   *   *

I agree that societies, like individuals, can be judged (up to a point) by their attitude towards beggars, and in that connection I remember my old friend and sometime enemy, Bandi Havas, (his antics in exile and ultimate death in the cellars of the Secret Police I have described elsewhere.)

We were strolling together in Casablanca one day in 1940

when we passed a beggar who looked particularly starved even by Moroccan standards. As this was a prosperous period for me, *i.e.,* I was eating fairly regularly for the first time in over two years, I gave the man a coin and was immediately landed on by Havas, a life-long Marxist with decided views on the coming world revolution. "You Social Democrats are sentimental fools," he said with real outrage in his voice. "You'll never understand that only revolution can remove hunger and that the hungrier these beggars get the angrier they'll become and the sooner we'll have the revolution!"

There have been many revolutions in the world since that day in Casablanca, but I haven't noticed a decline in the number of beggars. In the meantime I've learned to distrust those who talk about their "love of the people" but merely spout theories when confronted with misery. In my experience those most vocal about their love of humanity are the least likely to feed the hungry, or for that matter to say good morning to a stranger in an elevator. On the other hand, I have never seen Jacqueline, who has no political or social theories, or E., who is a complete nihilist philosophically, ever pass a beggar without automatically giving something.

June 8

Whoever designed this cottage either forgot or did not believe in lavatories. The existing one is small, unwired, and tacked onto the rest of the structure so half-heartedly that one awaits the gust of wind, slammed door, or one-flush-too-many that will one day send it hurtling into the little ravine below.

It's rather romantic, though, with three candle-stubs in a cigar box full of sand, one tiny window with spider-webs for a curtain, and a tall stack of back issues of *Time*. The only part of that publication I have ever fully trusted is the obituary column, and from this I have learned that Robert Payne died four years ago as did, more recently, Jiddu Krishnamurti.

I met Payne for about ten seconds some years ago when I was teaching at Columbia University in New York. A mutual acquaintance said that he would like to meet me, so a rendezvous was arranged at a campus restaurant. In those days I shared a tiny office across the hall from the much grander quarters of a not-yet-notorious Zbigniew Brezinski, and from there the acquaintance and I crossed the campus, past a mob of students who were chanting to mourn the death of Ho Chi Minh. We were laughing about something or other and so were challenged by angry demonstrators. "I don't mourn dead politicians," I said, and pushed through the crowd. A few feet away was Payne, who had watched the scene. We shook hands and then, with acute embarrassment, he said that he could not stay just now but would be happy to meet me some other time. My companion later said that Payne was the shiest man he had ever met; but that hardly accounts for the incident, which puzzles me yet. Nor can I believe that the author of *Chungking Diary* was afraid of antagonizing the loudmouths who dominated the student body of Columbia in those days.

Time's obituary notice, in its characteristically tasteless and pseudo-sophisticated manner, manages to suggest that his fame was small but greater than he deserved. Well, many of Payne's books were carelessly written and betray more enthusiasm than judgement. But at his best, as in *Chungking Diary*, that almost adolescent enthusiasm and exaggeration bathes his subjects in the light of love, and the effect is memorable. Reading that document one would give a lot to have been there in his company.

Time was kinder, or perhaps just more cautious, with Krishnamurti, who died recently in his tenth decade. Krishnamurti's appeal is felt less often among the disaffected young and the cult-seekers than among middle-aged, middle-class, intelligent, and thoughtful professionals—the intellectual elite of *Time*-subscribers, and so immune from attack.

I first heard Krishnamurti's name as a teenager in Budapest in the 1920s. He must have visited the city, for I remember his photograph in a newspaper: a Greek god with a black face, and eyes of a lambency even newsprint could not dim. I will not pretend that the two books of his I later read did any more than move and puzzle me. And yet, reading them, one could vaguely imagine a human race at peace with itself and the rest of creation, a turning away from names to confront things in themselves, a freedom from the rubbish-laden stream of emotion that usually passes for thought among us.

An obituary notice that was not news to me was that of Tennessee Williams, whom I met once in Tangier and (to ignore the injunction *de mortuis nihil nisi bunkum*) had no desire to meet again. This was in the days when Princess Aisha, the sister of Hassan II (sword of Allah, defender of the poor, tin-pot dictator), used to sit in a nightclub near the grand Socco, her Ton-Ton Macoute bodyguards strategically placed nearby. At another table one was likely to find on occasion Paul Bowles, Brian Gyson, William Burroughs, and/or any number of lesser lights come to Tangier to soak up the at-mosphere, a mixture of '20s Berlin and Timbuktu.

Into all this one day strode Tennessee Williams, who promptly begged of Rory, a friend of mine, that she "get him a boy." Being a woman of the world, Rory shrugged and rang up the U.S. Air Base near Kenitra, and some hours later a young American arrived and went off, happily one hopes, with the lustful playwright.

Everybody has a Tennessee Williams story, and E. once told me how in the spring of 1966, when he was spending a week in Taormina, living in a sleeping bag in the ruins of a church beside the San Domenico Palace Hotel, he awoke one morning to see Williams and his secretary Bill Galvin walking in the adjacent gardens. Hailing them, he was invited to dinner that evening on the strength of a previous meeting with Williams in Chicago.

Throughout dinner, at a table outdoors on the Corso, Williams took pills with almost every sip of wine. He was very far gone when, unexpectedly, an American Negro, an acquaintance of Galvin's approached them and, to cover up his shyness, went into one of those routines that not even a vibrant Afro-American can always bring off: "No! Don't tell me! Surely it's not..!" and so on.

"I don't have to take this shit," said Williams quietly. "Go on, get out of here." The boy, understandably, left. As did E., as soon as he possibly could.

Most Tennesse Williams stories tend to be of this sort, but obviously there was more to the man than drugs and brutal bad manners. This century has few if any playwrights who can, in my opinion, match his improbably credible dialogue for all its Gothic camp, or his ability to create a total atmosphere out of that dialogue. Hamlet was never so firmly on Danish soil as Blanche DuBois was in New Orleans. Mexico figures scarcely at all in *The Night of the Iguana*, yet it haunts the piece, as strangely unforgettable as the characters themselves. How did he do it? I don't know; but it's a question one asks only about very great writers.

*   *   *

One is, at heart, an animist: Eating a melon this morning I again felt the small urge that has been with me since childhood, to take one seed outdoors and plant it so that its family should not die out.

*   *   *

Struggling this afternoon with some lines about George Lukács, the Hungarian political commissar and Marxist theorist, the anniversary of whose death I like to celebrate every year with a few acerbic lines, I was reminded suddenly of the following passage in Josef Pieper's *Musse und Kult* and looked it up: "A man who is caught up and entangled in the web of everyday life may nevertheless one day be shaken by some deep emotion, whether it comes to him in the form of a philosophical question, a poem, or a face; but a sophist, a pseudo-philosopher, can never be shaken." Philosophically Lukács was never shaken by anything except a change in the party line, at which point he never failed to jump through whatever new hoops his masters held up.

*   *   *

Some characters in literature one would like to have dinner with: Alyosha and Ivan Karamazov, Grushenka, Felix Krull, Scheherezade, Nikolka Turbin, the Abbé Coignard, Encolpius, Frau Chauchat, Settembrini.

Some who would definitely not be invited: Emma Bovary, Fyodor Pavlovich Karamazov, Hans Castorp, Anna Karenina, Thomas Buddenbrooks, Becky Sharp, Anne of Green Gables.

June 9

There is a place beyond the ravine where, after this morning's deluge, there was a miniature waterfall, fantastic in its Japanese-garden way of replicating a larger world. I stared awhile, half expecting Rimbaud's rabbit to appear beneath a rainbow, then walked in the wet grass beside the road to Mrs. McN.'s general store. I had a vague notion of phoning Toronto, but when I got there the phone booth was occupied by a hefty lady apparently telling the story of her life with great urgency to someone at the other end. I thumbed through a magazine and finally left for home with the word "Shalimar" lingering idly in my mind from an advertisement.

I've forgotten what was advertised, but Shalimar is clearly the name of a small, isolated country lying somewhere between Burgundy and Kosovo. It is a rather more charming place to live in than Auden's utopia. The language of government is Provençal (with Latin on solemn occasions); politically it is a timocracy, and candidates for office must undergo yearly, Mandarin-style examinations in music, poetry, mathematics, commonsense, and kindness, the top-scorer being King or Queen for the year; agriculture is the chief industry, no machines being allowed except those driven by wind or water-power; transportation is by foot, horse, or oxen-pulled railway; there are no newspapers, radio, or television; literacy is universal, but printing forbidden: Anyone wishing to own a book must copy it out by hand (which effectively separates the sheep from the goats at both ends of *that* business); no music later than Schubert is allowed on the reasonable grounds that nothing before him is really bad and nothing after him indisputably good; the body of law, known as the *Codex Caritatis*, is based on the principle that nothing is criminal except that which is cruel or unkind; exile is the severest form of punishment; immigration, of course, is not allowed.

*   *   *

The postman arrived with an extraordinarily large bundle of mail and asked me, half seriously, if I was running a mail-order business. Rather unwisely I replied, half seriously, that considering Canada Post's record of delivery, it would be a very hazardous undertaking. Taking this in good part, he mentioned that he was attacked recently by a bull. I'm too old myself to run very fast nowadays, so I asked him where this had happened. It turned out, however, that a pit bull is not, as I had assumed, a bovine animal employed in mines, but a savage dog which Canadians (he claims) regularly turn loose on posties. I gave him a cup of coffee, but when he asked me what I was "into," and I told him "making poems," he seemed embarrassed, possibly frightened, and soon left. Perhaps Robin Skelton has been here before, and convinced everybody that poets are witches and warlocks.

*   *   *

E., although of origins so excessively Aryan a Nazi would have envied them, is a partisan of all things Jewish (except, curiously, the State of Israel) and vowed recently never again to set foot in Austria so long as "that man" is its president. Now he has been fishing with Yugoslav friends at a lake near the Drava and writes that they all drove to Austria to buy sturdier tackle for a huge fish called the Amurska (introduced from Siberia).

> I got out of the car on the Yugoslav side and waited while the others drove to a town called Leibnitz to shop. A militia man on guard asked me why I had not accompanied them, and I said: "It's full of Nazis over there." He laughed, glanced around, and replied: "Over here too." I have never before seen a militia man laugh. It was a bit alarming.

Once I suggested to him that he write a guide book entitled *The Europe I Love*, for he is passionately attached to a few places and knows them in amazing detail. But the map accompanying this guide book would look very odd, showing nothing but a few places in Spain, Italy, Finland, and Holland west of the Iron Curtain, the rest mostly blank and probably marked *Terra inhabitabilis* and *Hic sunt dracones*. The East Block would be better represented, the only countries he generally avoids in his wanderings over there being Poland and Hungary "because they're full of anti-Semites," people who "on the rare occasions they're not talking about money are cursing the Jews for being obsessed with it." It's a narrow view, but not entirely groundless.

*   *   *

On the way back to the cottage today, a car stopped beside me, a young tourist from Calgary with his family. They asked for directions, which I could not give them, but they gave me a ride anyway. He is a Vietnam veteran, now happily Canadian, but, as he told me, still suffering not so much from the trauma of combat as from a permanent horror of "what we did over there" for no very apparent purpose.

One of the things I like about America is the way its citizens—not often perhaps, but not so rarely as the citizens of most countries—try to look at themselves honestly.

This is very different from the inability of many Europeans to acknowledge any possible personal or national short-comings, so different that the rest of the world is apt to put it down to American *naïveté*.

If you talk with the older generation of Germans, as I often have, about World War II, you are likely to hear at nauseating length all about their sufferings in 1945-46 (which were, God knows, real enough) with never the slightest mention of the fact that they brought those sufferings upon themselves by following Hitler—not to mention that they were small com-pared with the appalling misery, the sheer obscene horror of their crimes against the rest of Europe.

Russian dissidents are, with a few honourable exceptions, another group of sufferers who seem unaware that their tragedy is home-grown, and that they are not its only victims. One looks in vain through most Russian dissident writing for any recognition of the fact that ten East European countries have been gagged and bled dry by Mother Russia in recent history. One suspects that they share Dostoyevsky's view that the nation requires and deserves an empire, though of course it should not be Marxist. The awful thing, to them, is that *Russians* are imprisoned and enslaved. It seems to have oc-curred to almost none of them—as it occurred to that Ameri-can tourist—that countries, so long as they are not occupied by foreign armies, are responsible for their own actions, and that conceivably they get the governments they deserve.

When Voltaire shouted, "Ecrasez l'infâme!" it was as a Frenchman with other Frenchmen particularly in mind. Mr. Solzhenitsyn's troubles might have come from invading Martians, so little responsibility does he place on the shoul-ders of Mother Russia.

June 10

After struggling most of the afternoon to translate (from E.'s English crib and notes) a really wonderful poem of

Georgi Ivanov, a lyrical nihilist who died in exile in France in 1958, I gave it up temporarily and took a walk. Half-way to the pond the whole thing suddenly fell into place and I scurried back to the cottage for paper and pencil. Four hours later it became as good as I'm likely to make it.

Afterwards, burrowing further into my host's splendid library, I discovered a German section between the bed and the wall, down by the floorboards. Creeping along like a mouse, I came across Barker Fairley's Heine, then a complete Heine, Rilke in his opaque and dubious Orphic period, and finally someone unknown to me, one Johannes Bobrowski, whose books have wonderful titles like *The Lithuanian Klavier* and *Lewin's Mill*.

He turns out unexpectedly to have been a Christian poet in East Germany who "lived quietly in a tiny, book-lined house in Berlin-Lichtenberg, where he died after a brief illness at an early age." Bobrowski was a prisoner of war in the Soviet Union for some years after 1945, and the first thing I noticed in his poems was their total lack of Russophobia. In the most wretched of conditions he found things and people to love. An admirable, remarkable man.

The poems, to my intense regret, do not seem to me as remarkable as their author. They are what everybody calls "modern" for lack of another adjective. That is to say, they are formless, with a lovely coherence of sense but without any discernible rhythm, music or shape—eerily evocative prose broken (apparently at random) into uneven lines and strewn down the page. But having said that, I must add that they *are* evocative and the contents are memorable even if the words are not. Nevertheless, I shall still be insisting on my deathbed that one of the things that separates poetry from language in its other manifestations is a memorable, soaring architecture of musical and magical words. No one would claim that Christian Morgenstern's *Galgenlieder* is great poetry, but no one who has read his *Möwenlied*, for example, will ever entirely forget "*Die Möwen sehen alle aus/als ob sie Emma hiessen* (which means simply that "All seagulls look as if they were named Emma"). That, like Ogden Nash, is verse so light, so buoyed up on laughing gas, that it floats straight to the ceiling; but you don't easily forget it, for all that. Someone once said that many books are undeservedly forgotten, but none are undeservedly remembered. The same, surely, goes for poems.

Bobrowski was one of the very few non-Balt poets to have been preoccupied with that slate-grey part of the world known as Balticum, the Northern end of the great Sarmatian plain and stretching, roughly, from Leningrad to Pskov to Travemünde. He loved bare Lutheran churches, Latvian folk songs, Russian villages, midsummer-night festivals on the amber-strewn Baltic shores. *Utinam requiescat apud Deum suum.*

* * *

A huge full moon is hanging over the treetops tonight like a Chinese lantern, far superior to the moon one sees (how rarely!) in the murky glow over night-time Toronto.

There is something faintly wrong about a moon over an urban landscape, some suspicion of commercialism, as if the thing were really a disguised Goodyear blimp or an advertising gimmick. Walking over a railway bridge in Budapest with a friend one night, I stopped to admire a wonderfully red moon—which suddenly turned green, revealing itself as a semaphore down the line.

* * *

Once the shock of arrest subsides, it is a great relief in a Communist country to find yourself in a prison cell: Paradoxically you feel free at last to be yourself. Also there is the fact that many thousands share the same fate; and misery, after all, does love company. For a poet to be arrested in the USA would be a personal and perhaps professional catastrophe, as would be a sentence of exile to the USSR. But for an East European, such experiences, although calamities, are not all that unusual and, if he survives them, spiritually and artistically useful.

I think this phenomenon, the comparative ease with which one accepts a more or less common fate, explains a lot in the history of literature. Throughout the golden age of Chinese poetry, from the T'ang to the Sung dynasties, the normal lot of many of the best poets was exile, poverty or, at best, official disfavour. Yet poets from the superlative (but, sadly, little known) Li Ho to the more famous Su Tung-P'o never complain about their fates as being anything out of the way. Instead of howls of outrage (imagine Allen Ginzberg jailed in Moscow or Blagoveshchensk!) there is merely a clear-eyed recognition of the situation, a certain wistfulness and, as if floating on clouds high above the wretched earth, page after page of serenely contemplative lyricism. Perhaps it is not so much that misery loves company, as that when his world is divided between the oppressors and the oppressed, a real poet in any country is instinctively consoled to find himself on the better side and, sustained by the good company of many fellow sufferers, able to make use of his pain. One is either crushed or rises to new heights. Howls are of no use to anyone.

*   *   *

It's normally fatal for a poet to become fanatically converted to a ready-made *Weltanschauung*, whether religious, philosophical, or political. A terrible example is Mayakovsky, famous in the West—though no more talented than two now-forgotten German socialist poets of the 19th century, Georg Herwegh and Ferdinand Freiligrath. In his pre-Marxist days, Mayakovsky wrote some very good things, including his famous and durable poem about the death of a starved and frozen horse in a Petersburg street. Later as a Marxist, he couldn't be bothered to notice that people were dying around him from the same causes, and his poems from that period read now, seven decades later, like gallows humour.

*   *   *

Why is it that wine tastes better from a crystal goblet than from an earthenware cup? Why would the tea that I am drinking at the moment taste better had I brought my own bone china cup with me? E. maintains this belief in the ameliorating properties of objects to the point of insisting that his Ibis typewriter—bought for ninety-eight dollars in Yugoslavia and looked after with a care most people reserve for their sports cars—writes better poems than any word processor.

June 11

Poring over Roloff Beny's *In Italy*, my mind floated back to my first solitary journey at the age of sixteen. This was in 1926 when Florence, my goal, had changed less in four centuries than it has in the intervening sixty years. I arrived late at night, but instead of looking for a room, I sat in a doorway across from the Baptistry and until dawn watched mesmerized as the moonlight played on the surface of that extraordinary building. Sometime during the night a rather charming prostitute, thinking me homeless, brought me a coffee and, sitting chastely beside me, delicately answered my bashful questions about her profession. At first light, when the shopkeepers and coffeehouse proprietors emerged to prepare for business, they cast understanding smiles in my direction. It was taken for granted that a young man might do worse than spend a night contemplating Florence in the moonlight.

The last time my wanderings took me through Florence, things had of course changed. The people of Italy are *au fond* among the kindest in the world, but the smiles are wearing thin nowadays, and in a Florence overrun by tens of thousands of young people attending a rock festival, faces verged on the grim. One paid five dollars for a cup of coffee, punk-styled prostitutes had become indistinguishable from the female university students, and as the moonlight poured down upon that same Baptistry there came a distant rhythmical, electronically amplified roaring and what sounded like the clash of spears upon shields. In 1926 one would have taken that noise for the return of the Goths, accompanied this time by Zulu auxiliaries—and one would not have been far off the mark.

* * *

It was in 1924 or '25 that my parents took me to Naples and Pompeii. Looking now at a book called *Eros in Pompeii*, I can contemplate for the first time those "shocking" statues and frescos once forbidden to the eyes of women and adolescents. Like most Roman art, these have a slightly puzzling, unsettling charm: It is clearly an early state of our own world, but seen through very foreign eyes. The Greek view of things, oddly, is rather closer to us.

At fifteen, an age when the merest hint of the erotic usually sets the pulse pounding, I remember that what *was* shown to me (a few nymphs and satyrs and the ubiquitous good-luck signs of erect phalluses) registered in my imagination as anything but sexual. The strange truth is that there was no, or almost no, pornography in our antiquity. That fresco on the wall of a brothel showing a rather nervous young man about to penetrate a girl *à la vache* has an inscription reading: *Impelle Lente*. Enter slowly. Clearly it was not intended to arouse the clientele, but to protect the staff. It's all very Roman, which is to say, matter-of-fact. Even that mutilated masterpiece, the *Satyricon* of Petronius, though steeped in sex from beginning to end, is not pornographic; indeed, it is marvelously comic in just those passages where no modern author could have avoided lubricity. A "cool chasteness" hovers over Roman obscenity, and to be aroused by it one would have to be in the throes of a particularly difficult puberty.

Nowadays it is usually assumed that the bedroom frescos were painted to inflame jaded passions. I wonder. It is easy to imagine a happily married Roman couple—Maximus Lascivius, let us say, and his wife Laetitia Matutina—lying abed and looking in the lamplight at the catalogue of erotic possibilities in much the same way their cook looked at the dining room frescos as a sort of menu. "How about that one in the corner, Maxi? The one where Paria has got her leg sort of around the neck of what's-his-name?" "Right," replies Maximus in the tones of one who has decided on stuffed quail instead of another helping of nightingale tongues. "Let's give it a try. *Impellam lente*."

        *   *   *

My son Andrew, who lives in England, mentions in a letter some older people he knows who "pretend that they enjoyed the Blitz during the war." What makes him think they're pretending?

When you consider that the average wage-earner is forced by industrialized society to spend his days performing tasks that would drive a monkey mad in a week, and that for most people life after adolescence consists largely of toil, anxiety, brief pleasures, extended pains, endless pretense, and ultimate disillusion—when you consider all this, and more, you will not be surprised that many people secretly exulted when the whole deadly process was suddenly interrupted and life became, for a moment, filled with danger, excitement, passion, and intense friendships.

My friend George Mikes tells me that strangers spoke to one another during the Blitz—something almost unheard of before it—and that people generally allowed themselves to be human with one another, sometimes even forgetting class distinctions. My God, if I were a London labourer or office worker, I would not only be nostalgic for the Blitz but probably praying for another one.

June 12

There was a strange little episode of *déjà vu* this morning after I made the forty-minute trek to the store for groceries and a treat of that metallic Canadian chocolate that's like biting into deliciously flavoured tinfoil. On the way back I suddenly realized that my wallet, which held all my money for the next six weeks, was missing.

The last time that happened was over a quarter of a century ago, in Bolzano, where I had gone with Suzy, who was terminally ill with cancer. Leaving her to rest in the hotel, I had gone out for medicine and various other things, when in the middle of the street I found that my wallet was missing. It contained over five-hundred pounds sterling, an enormous sum for a refugee in those days. It was meant to cover not only hotels and meals but also doctors for Suzy. Stunned, almost blinded by despair, I was leaning against a wall when a middle-aged Italian, an assistant in the last shop I had visited, came running up and handed me the wallet, fat with five-pound notes. "You forgot this, signor," he said with a smile, and adamantly refused a reward.

There was no wall to lean on this morning, and I was consoling myself that this time at least the loss affected no one but myself, when suddenly the teenaged son of Mrs. McN. came round the bend on his bicycle and handed me the wallet with a huge smile. He did not refuse a reward— he was off again into the wind before I even had time to offer one.

Weighed down with more years and the memory of more horrors than one had bargained for in the beginning, one is tempted so often to a settled view that the world is cruel and people, for the most part, bad. And then somebody comes racing up with your lost wallet, happy to have made you happy.

*   *   *

We *are* what we *do*. What we do and the spirit in which we do it, no matter what our position in the world, seems to determine whether we enjoy and disseminate some measure of happiness or (the only alternative) it were better we had never been born.

*   *   *

"To ask what life means is like asking what music means. It's just there, and is happy, or the opposite of happy, depending largely upon the quality of our contemplation of it. There is no happiness without contemplation, and neither happiness nor contemplation without acceptance of the world as it is."

—*Bernd von Bellingshausen*

*   *   *

Some major poets I have tried and failed to like: Pindar, Lucretius, Virgil, Milton, Pope, Dryden, Goethe, Pushkin, Petöfi, Shelley, Tennyson.

Some minor ones I love: Petronius, Li Ho (791-817 A.D.), Gottschalk of Orbais (ca. 808-868 A.D.), Ikkyu Sojun (1394-1481 A.D.), Michelangelo Buonarroti, Du Bellay, Sor Juana Ines de la Cruz (16th century Mexican), Carl-Michael Bellman, Robert Burns.

*   *   *

Countries whose customs officers, in my experience, are apt to make one feel like a criminal: Hungary, Yugoslavia, France, England, Morocco, Canada. It's puzzling that Canada should have to be included in this unpleasant list, for the average Canadian does not *normally* turn into a petty tyrant the moment he puts on a uniform.

June 13

An owl has been hooting not far away again this evening, and one fears for the small creatures out there, "the furry and the obtuse," as Christina Rossetti called them. Back in Toronto Jacqueline is (I hope and trust) looking after the nine tiny finches who inhabit my bedroom and who delight in dive-bombing guests (though when the Toronto *Star* came to photograph them one day they all retired to the inner branches of their trees and refused to come out).

Pigeons also like my apartment and spend a lot of time in small groups on the balcony. One day several years ago a hawk of some sort, bigger than I had known a bird could get, swooped down there. All the pigeons scattered except for one who huddled paralyzed with fear beneath a chair. E. grabbed a large kitchen knife, flung open the balcony door and confronted the creature (whose wingspan was wider than the balcony itself) which, after several uncomfortable seconds, flew off. Hawks have to live too, of course, but as they're not endearingly furry and obtuse, one is unfairly inclined to drive them off. But we were never promised that the world was fair.

*　　　*　　　*

The CBC news is going on and on about Free Trade. Each time I hear the phrase I feel a vague, perhaps irrational fear that this place I'm inhabiting at the moment will disappear once the door is opened to "progress" and unshackled "development." Nobody likes to say it aloud, but of all the good things about Canada, one of the best is that it is definitely not the United States.

Does anyone know exactly what Free Trade will mean? It's clear the government does not. My private fear is that it will mean that Vancouver Island will come to resemble Coney Island. What then will happen to the furry and the obtuse?

> "They will answer confidentially
> as to a privileged clientele,
> that death, my people, death
> as the native poet warns us
> 'death goes better with Coca-Cola.'"
> —*Marya Fiamengo,*
> *"Notes from an Intellectual Branch Plant"*

*　　　*　　　*

Ever since reading Al Purdy's anthology *The New Romans* shortly after I arrived in Canada in 1967, I have observed the phenomenon of Canadian anti-Americanism without altogether understanding it. When it is real (as opposed to being a collective knee-jerk), it seems to be a form of sibling rivalry, a family relationship in which little brother's whole identity is threatened by the worldly success, notoriety, size, and wounding lack of concern on the part of big brother. It is also possible that some of those born in Canada simply feel, as I do, that many of the essential differences between the two countries are worth fighting to preserve—such as the Canadian tendency towards obeying the law; expecting (if not always getting) honesty in government institutions; a horror of loud-mouthed self-advertisement and the more tiresome forms of nationalism; keeping most of the country happily underdeveloped. American influence seems to me an indisputable threat to all of these things, one way or another.

The larger phenomenon of international anti-American-ism, which has mildly intrigued me for over half a century now, is still more difficult to analyze. Looking into my own heart, I find a certain admiration for the USA and its people: No country has ever been as generous; its inhabitants are among the friendliest, by and large, and most hospitable to be found anywhere, and they enjoy a fantastic degree of liberty, bordering at times on anarchy. One is tempted at times to love them, but they are already doing that well enough themselves.

Ever since I first landed in America in 1941, my admiration has been tempered by a large admixture of contempt. It is, after all, not Marxism but what is known as "Americanism" that has in my lifetime utterly destroyed the ancient culture I love deeply: the tradition of humane learning, the society of humanism moving slowly and painfully century after century upwards towards justice, *paideia* and ever-higher achievement, while keeping greed, opportunism and the merely banausic in their places.

As long as I have known it, America has tended to view the rest of the world without any serious effort at intelligent understanding, and has interfered with it the way an over-grown child might, with presumption, good intentions, and perennial amazement at the sad results. While admiring many things about Americans, Europeans in particular are apt to shrink from them at the same time as from cynical innocents in possession of dangerous power. That they have sometimes used that power more wisely than Europeans have indeed, have twice saved Europe from its own madness—does nothing to alter the impression.

Thomas Mann once said that "Americans are the best Europeans." From one point of view, that of civil courage and the love of liberty, they are. From several other points of view, they are not Europeans at all, but merely a people living amidst the borrowed forms of European civilization without any serious interest in or understanding of those forms, in spite of the fact these are the only ones they have. It is certainly not that the average American is less intelligent or even less edu-cated than his European counterpart—as a lecturer I have often found him, as an audience, seemingly better endowed in both categories. The trouble is that the average is normally *all* one finds. Only in America is mediocrity—always and every-where the rule in this world—raised to the level of cult and positively admired. (Canada has managed somehow to escape this fate. An American friend from the University of North Carolina once mentioned to me that a man of Pierre Trudeau's intelligence, erudition, and style couldn't be elected dog-catcher in his state.) That something resembling the way of life of such a country should now be forced on the rest of us as the only alternative to Marxism-Leninism is enough to drive the most sanguinely tolerant, gymnasium-educated European to fury and despair.

June 14

Jacqueline has, perhaps in error, included a copy of the Vatican periodical *Latinitas* in a bundle of mail, an issue containing a poem by E., who has earned something of a reputation in that tiny group of people around the world who still write in Latin.

He is understandably a little tired of the amused incredulity with which the Latinless (most people nowadays) greet this passion of his, and once listed for me Five Good Reasons for Writing in Latin. These are: "1) You do not have to worry about the intelligence of your readers. They're bright. 2) Having gone to the trouble of learning a dead language, they are likely to be people who can think for themselves, not part of any herd. 3) Latin is at least sixteen centuries older than English and may yet outlive it. 4) Small is beautiful. Crafting a Latin poem is like engraving an intaglio. The result, if successful, is exquisite and permanent. 5) It is intellectual resistance against the general rot. Like the Hasidim and the Amish, one is saying *No* to all the trivial crap of modern life."

Even when not making polemical lists, E. can be a bit testy on the subject. I once asked him if it was not discouraging, writing in such a little-known language. "That's a rather odd question," he replied, "coming from a Hungarian poet." On another occasion a quite talented Canadian poetess, tipsy at the moment, made the mistake of asking him if "anyone who really had anything to say would say it in Latin." Smiling slightly and pouring the lady another drink, E. replied gently: "You're not likely to find out, are you?"

For my part, I have never seriously considered writing verse in anything but my native Hungarian. On the other hand, there is something to be said for E.'s attitude. An old friend of mine, the late Alexander Lenard, quite unexpectedly hit the bestseller list some years ago with his Latin version of A.A. Milne's *Winnie the Pooh*. A Hungarian refugee, Lenard had found himself living in the wilds of Brazil. As a physician he treated the ailments of local settlers and was paid with chickens, sides of ham, and eggs. For seven years, to keep his sanity, he painstakingly translated that little book into what is probably the smoothest and most amusing humanistic Latin ever devised. On a lecture tour of South America I asked him what had possessed him to learn Latin to that degree of excellence, and he told me.

During World War II, which he spent as a refugee hiding from the Gestapo in Rome, it became clear to him that he was not living in the best of centuries. As it was also the least literate of centuries as regards serious literature, he decided that the one place the authorities would never look for a fugitive from Fascist justice was in a first-rate library. From then on, to earn his daily bread, he illegally treated his Italian neighbours' high blood-pressure and so on, and then would slip into a large monastic library where for the rest of the day, for many hundreds of days, he read all there was to read there, Latin. "Every afternoon I entered the Middle Ages, a blessed relief after the Rome of 1944," he said, and added a remark I have always cherished: "The library is the head-office of European civilization." He became so happy in this atmosphere in spite of hunger, danger, and privation that when the war ended he decided to continue "reading nothing written after the French Revolution, except of course medical journals."

A man of many talents, Lenard won a contest on Brazilian TV playing Bach fugues on the organ. With the prize money he had his translation, *Winnie ille Pu*, typeset in Sao Paulo by a Hungarian on the machinery of an Italian-language daily. "A typically Hungarian business," as he said. Eventually a Swedish and then a British publisher took a chance on it, and before long Oxford students were mobbing Blackwell's to get a copy. It sold well over a hundred thousand copies and Lenard built himself a modest little house at the edge of the jungle where, until his death in 1970, he read Petronius and listened to Bach. Robert Graves—no mean Latinist himself—wrote an introduction to Lenard's autobiography, *The Valley of the Latin Bear.*

"Over a hundred thousand copies?" asked E., taken aback, when I first told him about Lenard. He looked thoughtful for a moment, then, more at war with the century of *Massenmensch* than even Lenard was, he replied: "I'd take the money, of course...but then start writing in Sanskrit. *Very* few people know Sanskrit."

*   *   *

One of North America's Hungarian newspapers has a neo-Spenglerian article on the decline of the West, written by a gentleman who is himself evidence of that decline. He laments the passing of the good old days, by which he means the era of Admiral Horthy's White Terror, Jew-baiting, a half-starved peasantry, and a rapacious, cretinous ruling class. He most emphatically does not mean the minority Hungary of liberal aspirations, Social Democracy, classical education, and attempts at social justice. Towards the end of his diatribe he goes on about the "three bestial perversions now widely tolerated in the West, homosexuality, lesbianism, and heterosexuality." There is nothing like a certain kind of Hungarian editorial to leave one smiling the rest of the day.

Apropos the good old days, it is true that there was a time when that sort of imbecility would never have got into print. There were—and presumably still are—people in Hungary steeped and mellowed in civilization. The gymnasium I attended in Budapest throughout much of my youth represented a cross-section of the population, with the admittedly enormous exclusion of the extremely poor. The older I become the more I realize the excellence of the instruction there: year after year of Latin, Greek, history, and literature. It all seemed somewhat pointless at the time, and yet when I look at the fates of the dozens of young men who graduated with me—fates known from the reports reaching me of regular class reunions—only one of them came to a disgraceful end, a surly youth who became an announcer on Radio Kiev during the Nazi occupation of the Soviet Union during the war. He was hanged in 1945, a year of enormous crimes and occasional small justices. *None* of

48

my other classmates ever became either a Nazi or a Communist.

The point is, I think, that for a man who has been in prolonged contact with the best his civilization has to offer—whether he be a Chinese Confucianist, a Hungarian Greek scholar, or a sixth-former under Mister Chips—it is hard to sink to the level of Radio Kiev (Nazi or Soviet) or to yellow-press journalism. Recent history has more than amply proved that the average scientist, brought up on a more modern intellectual diet and then employed by the state, is by comparison a moral lap-dog, ready to jump on command. Which proves, if my logic is correct, that science is not, as usually assumed, the most valuable thing our civilization has produced.

*   *   *

"Ill fares the land, to hastening ills a prey,
Where Science accumulates, and Men decay."
—Goldsmith

June 15

About a mile from here a young couple with a golden-haired infant daughter have built a sort of Hobbit-house beside a huge, moss-covered oak. There is also a dogwood tree nearby and beds of daffodils. They seem to be the contemporary, much improved version of what used to be called hippies, that is, kids who have rejected middle-class backgrounds in favour of simplicity, tranquility, and peace. The young man rides a horse, hoes the large garden by hand, and has built a loom. When they gave me camomile tea and we chatted at a table before the house, I noticed that their clothing was homespun. No great intellectual pursuits going on in that household, as far as one can tell; but then why should there be?

I happened to mention them at Mrs. McN.'s, and the

comments that came back, though not exactly derogatory, were vaguely disapproving. A man I had never seen before said, as he was leaving: "They're just running away from reality."

Now the man who said this was wearing what appeared to be a one hundred percent acrylic jump-suit, and one doubts that even his socks or underwear were made of anything Mother Nature would have recognized as her own. Outside he got into his car and roared off in a cloud of squandered and non-renewable resources. It left me asking myself (rhetorically) whether a horse, which is alive, has less reality than a mobile heap of metal, glass, and vinyl. A society that thinks so, that prefers the dead and artificial in everything from food to transportation, is not only out of touch with reality but might fairly be described as sick.

*　　*　　*

Why do North American so often say, especially in reference to a more or less public figure, "He is a personal friend of mine"? Do they have any impersonal friends?

*　　*　　*

Thanks to the necessarily thin spread of a pre-packaged universal education and the rise of mass media, we are now living in an age of cant, with a body of received "truth" larger than any 13th-century scholastic could have dreamed of. Among the things held to be self-evident are the innate and eternal superiority of democracy, the priority of rights before duties, the right of government to control such things as education and immigration (both largely up to the individual until fairly recently), and a universal belief in the curative powers of literacy.

It was, I believe, Rebecca West who once wrote that every writer worth his salt knows that only a fraction of what is printed ever begins to compensate the reader for the loss of the powers of memory and observation he has suffered by becoming literate. This was illustrated for me in

Morocco some years ago by a boy who was a gate-guard in a building complex just outside Tangier.

Abd-el-Aziz was about seventeen and totally illiterate. Sometimes when I left for my daily walk through the hills overlooking the Straits of Gibraltar, he would slip away from his post and accompany me a mile or so. Being unlettered, he had, by listening and imitating, taught himself a lot of French and Spanish, even a bit of German, and so could describe to me everything I was missing not only during my walks but in my life in Morocco itself. I was, and still am, ashamed to admit that Abd-el-Aziz saw two or three times more of the world about him than I did or do. He knew all the plants and their curative powers and an almost infinite number of stories and songs; and his easy ability to read the characters of people from their faces and movements filled me with astonishment. Once we passed a strolling European of my acquaintance, and on the basis of a minute's silent observation, Abd-el-Aziz, prompted by me, later described the man's character, his virtues and faults, with breathtaking accuracy. It wasn't idle speculation, but analysis of a type far beyond the powers of the average neo-Freudian quack.

Until recently most of the cultures of the world were carried on and added to by people like Abd-el-Aziz, for only a few, such as the European and the Chinese, have rested even in part on foundations of paper. These cultures are all rapidly dying out now. If Abd-el-Aziz has children they will almost certainly work at occupations as humble as his own, but instead of sitting at the gate noticing and remembering everything, they will read the mindless daily press or, more likely, comic books.

One of the best contemporary Moroccan writers, Mohammed Choukri, was illiterate until his twenties when he taught himself, with great effort, to read and write both Arabic and French. Late one night in the medina of Tangier many years ago, he told me sadly that if he had grown up literate he would never have become a writer. "I write now what I saw then. I can't see anymore, really. All I know is what I read." I know what he means.

*   *   *

I have not been back to Tangier for ten years now, and can't say that I miss it much, though it's played an important role in my life since I took refuge there in 1940. It was part of Spanish Morocco back then, and as notorious a "sin city" as Macao. But one had already seen and been bored by such sad flesh-pots as pre-Hitler Berlin, and it was friendship that for a long time drew me regularly back to Tangier: Lily K., Virginia and Alec Waugh, Princess Ruspoli, Ali the aged head waiter at the Café de Paris (who served me absinthe in 1940 and Coca-Cola in 1978), and other familiar faces, including Jim Wylie, approaching ninety the last time I saw him, who had already lived in Tangier at a time when Christians were still killed on sight a few miles inland. The English poet and memoirist Peter Levi mentions Jim Wylie in one of his books, but does not tell my favourite Wylie story, one that just about summed up life in Tangier.

Jim owned a beautiful old house once occupied by Samuel Pepys at the top of the Casbah and reached by a succession of narrow, winding, dirty, and unlit alleyways. Coming home from a party late one night, he had almost reached his doorstep when, as he rounded a corner, a burnoose-hooded figure reached out, grabbed him by the throat with one hand, and held a knife aloft with the other. *Donne-moi ton argent!"* snarled a gutteral voice. Then suddenly, the man gasped and stepped back in the moonlight. "Oh! Mr. Wylie! Allah forgive me, I thought you were a tourist!"

Should anyone think that Tangier in the third-quarter of the 20th century is not firmly in the grip of Islam, I offer the example of Tahir the taxi driver. This unsavoury looking but friendly young Berber had taken a liking to me and would frequently pick me up in his little Fiat when I was waiting for a bus to take me into or out of Tangier. At twenty-two, Tahir was the quintessential street Arab and, by his own account, an ex-thief, smuggler, boy prostitute, and outspoken despiser of all things Moroccan, including, very atypically, Islam. He spoke so much against religion, declaring himself an atheist, that I was astonished one day, as we drove past the English Church, when he asked me if I would take him inside it. I agreed.

The doors of the church, as it turned out, were locked, and we were about to walk away when the custodian emerged and asked what we wanted. He was visibly worried when I told him. It is a capital offence in Morocco to entice a Moslem away from Islam. Nevertheless, he allowed us a brief peek inside the building, and Tahir's curiosity was satisfied. As we walked back to the taxi he asked me why the building was locked up.

"Probably so no one will steal anything," I said. Then to be polite I added, "European hippies, for instance."

"No Moroccan would ever steal from a mosque, not even from a *Nazrani* church," said Tahir, visibly shocked.

"Why not?"

"Anyone who does that," he said very gravely, "always dies on the third day after the theft."

June 16

Two impressions of Beograd from E.:

> At night the restaurant of the Hotel Moskva is a sort of social centre for the swinging young, with a band playing that unintentionally mournful music I call "East Block Rock." An unshaven waiter sat me just a few feet from the music, and I was fascinated to notice that the saxophone player, a pretty girl in a pink evening gown, was wearing army boots underneath.
>
> Beograd railway station at four in the morning is one of the most desolate sights imaginable. The

darkened waiting room was jammed with hundreds of poor travellers sleeping all over their cardboard boxes and suitcases in drugged exhaustion. On the nearest platform stood a group of five young toughs in leather jackets, passing round a bottle and looking, like their counterparts everywhere, faintly menacing. Then an old man in near-rags shuffled up to me and asked sadly when there would be a train for Sarajevo. Looking it up in my little book, the *Vozni Red*, I told him. Then he asked me again, still more plaintively, and I realized helplessly that he was either mad or stunned by some grief. I was just trying to find out what I could do for him when two of the hooligan types approached, took him gently by the arms, and led him to a corner of the platform where another two crushed some cardboard boxes onto which they very carefully lowered him, as onto a bed. They have him a drink from their bottle, then gently eased his old brief-case under his head for a pillow. As they passed me one of them said: "He'll be all right now." Then they went back into a huddle on the platform and resumed their look of faint menace.

I was a little sorry when the Zagreb Express pulled in. I was beginning to like Beograd a lot.

*   *   *

In his far-flung adventures as the last representative (as far as one knows) of the mediaeval tribe of wandering scholars and Latin poets, E. more nearly than anyone else I know of demonstrates:

> "...the five reasons for travel given me by Sayyid Abdulla, the watchmaker: 'to leave one's troubles behind one; to earn a living; to acquire learning; to practise good manners; and to meet honourable men.'"
>
> —*Freya Stark,* A Winter in Arabia

June 17

Summer lightning off towards the Pacific last night. E. once
told me the Russian word for it, which I've forgotten: something tremendously evocative like *zapaval* or *zapitsa*. This
soundless lightning always impresses me more than the
usual thunderbolt variety. It's like an artillery battle in a
silent film, a celestial struggle, Valhalla versus Olympus,
Jukahainen raging against Jumala in the *Kalevala*.

Afterwards I had one of those dreams that have haunted
me from time to time since childhood, with enough death
symbols to fill the notebooks of half a dozen industrious
little Freudians: Nazis, Hungarian Secret Police goons,
border guards, Revenue Canada inspectors, you name it.
They caught me and put me in an electric chair, but when I
woke up in agony it was a charley-horse, not a million volts.
I will never learn not to drink Turkish coffee before going
to bed.

Something that I envy E., and the few other people I
know who share it, is their total freedom from any fear of
death (as opposed to dying, which E. admits may be unpleasant). I pointed out to him once that there is, on the
other hand, nothing like the fear of death to make life
singularly sweet. Like many of those who have been closest
to me, he is candidly and sometimes chillingly cynical on
the subject of life: "It's interesting for a visit, but I wouldn't
want to stay there forever." Such attitudes, like my own
dread of non-existence, seem to be life-long. Years ago,
before he finally dropped his ingrained Catholicism, we
were wandering through the cathedral of Valencia one afternoon and the subject of immortality came up: "Of course
I *believe* in it, he said, "though personally I would prefer
extinction." I was outraged by that remark to the point of
writing a sonnet about it. Later it came as a small revelation
to me that fear of death was not the only possible motive
behind religious belief. Some people cling to it to make the
idea of *life* tolerable.

The Russian word for summer lightning has suddenly flashed into my mind: *zarnitsa*. (Like that of most Hungarians, my Russian vocabulary is limited to a few words and expressions learned just after World War II: *"Germania kaput!" "You give wrist-watch!"* That sort of thing.)

*   *   *

It's natural to surround yourself with people who share your own interests: both my wives and most of my closest friends have preferred, as I do, poetry and painting to the other arts, and almost none, until E. and Jacqueline, have cared particularly for music. But friends share, and during the past twenty years E. has learned to like painting, and I, after much puzzlement, have learned how to enjoy quite a lot of music, most notably Mozart, with enough pleasure in fact to wonder sometimes if the power of music is not often greater than that of any other art.

In Yugoslavia recently, he coaxed my somewhat reluctant self to a concert performance of the *Concerto in D Minor for Three Pianos and Strings* of his god, J. S. Bach, performed in a monastery church by a girl and two boys from the Zagreb Conservatory. Bach is, I confess, generally too complex for my untrained ear. But as that concerto progressed into the third movement, I felt electricity running through the audience and, at the end, when they stood up to roar approval, the woman beside me had tears streaming down her face, and E., quite pale, sat slumped in his seat visibly shaken. My own chief emotion was envy. It's terrible to be offered so obviously great a joy and not know quite how to grasp it. An assiduous cultivator of my own gods— Michelangelo, Catullus, *et alii*—I'm not altogether sure that lightning bolts of quite that voltage are ever within their power to hurl.

When E. first travelled from his Black Forest village to Malta in 1966 to help me translate a book, his arrival was preceded by a correspondence in which he remarked that he was astonished that I did not like music. He laughed when I later asked him how he had divined that fact. "It's simple. In the 472 pages of your autobiography you don't mention it once." If I were writing that book today, it would be different. There would be a bit about music, and rather more about the chagrin I now feel at being excluded from its highest mysteries.

June 18

Tried all last evening to write a poem, but somehow it would not progress. If you attempt to hasten the birth of a poem the result, as in the case of a mortal child, will be unfortunate. Part of the problem was the pleasant but distracting hooting of the owl in the forest. With one ear preoccupied by that sound, all my rhymes seemed to be written by a Hungarian Hilaire Belloc. Finally, giving it up, I took from the shelves a book mysteriously entitled *Watership Down*. Discovering it to be a novel about rabbits (no one could write a good novel about rabbits!), I came close to putting it back, but fortunately did not.

Dawn was beginning to break when I finished the last page. Now the sun is passing overhead on its daily flight to Japan, and I wonder if the owl spent the night preying on bunnies. I shall never look at a rabbit again without sympathetic interest, and certainly never eat one.

The owner of this happy volume has tucked two British reviews in the back, dessert as it were after the feast. One is headed "Watership Potemkin"; the other, still more amusingly, "Warren Peace."

June 19

Endless fuss in the newspapers and radio about Nicaragua, with Americans as usual divided among themselves on the question of whether to support a vile regime of the right or a vile regime of the left. I am reminded of a similar universal taking of sides fifty years ago, during the Spanish Civil War.

In 1936, Budapest was talking about little else, and a group of us, young writers and assorted coffee-house intellectuals, were spending the afternoon in a loud debate over the relative merits of Franco and his Republican opponents. At the peak of the noisy discussion the great writer Karinthy walked into the room and listened to us awhile with something close to contempt on his face. During a lull he asked those present, very drily: "During the War of the Spanish Succession which of you would have been for Phillip V and which for Maximilian of Bavaria? And which of you thinks there would have been the slightest sense in making such a choice?"

In the ensuing half century of equally senseless and bloody squabbles, I have always remembered Karinthy and that afternoon. When confronted with two evils, the choice is simple: Reject both. It seems an obvious enough truth, yet one can count on the fingers of one hand the number of people one knows who believe it, really believe it.

*   *   *

When I telephoned Vancouver at the call-box in front of the store today, there was a lot of interference on the line, eerie distant voices. Almost all my life I have wondered when using the telephone if the thing was bugged. Often it was, though never, I suppose, in Canada. One night in the summer of 1956, I was talking on the phone with the writer George Páloczi-Horváth, when suddenly a woman's voice broke in, saying with cool politeness: "Speak more slowly, please." The Secret Police seldom gave themselves away so blatantly, and I would by now have begun to doubt my memory of the incident had Páloczi-Horváth not recorded it in his own writings. It was strangely encouraging to learn that they had to take our conversations down in *shorthand*—that one's enemies were, technologically speaking, still in the 19th century.

*   *   *

One thought of Karinthy always leads to another, and I suddenly remember the story of the run-in our greatest humorist had with, of all things, the Swedish Esperanto Society.

Karinthy, though not knowing a word of Esperanto, was, on the strength of his fame and his genius in the Hungarian language, made honorary president of the Hungarian Esperanto Society. A few years before the war, desperately ill with a brain tumour, he was taken to Stockholm where an operation was successfully performed. As he lay in bed one day, recuperating, a nurse suddenly ushered in three gentlemen, middle-aged Vikings dressed (as Swedes are on every conceivable occasion) in tuxedos, and bearing flowers. Bowing and introducing themselves in a language Karinthy later described as sounding like "Spanish with the personality removed," the gentlemen stepped forward and one of them unrolled a document, evidently a speech in the same language.

Nonplussed for a moment, Karinthy's usual inspiration came to his rescue. Smiling at the Swedes, he said something like *"Sum gratificado . . . sono felice . . . ach, du lieber Gott, ich habe's vergessen!"* And putting his hand to his temple in consternation, he explained in German that he had been warned that an operation of this sort might cause him to lose certain areas of memory.

The Swedes, overcome with compassion and concern, spoke gently to him in German and expressed their hope that the day would soon come when his memory of Esperanto returned. Somewhere in the archives of the Swedish Esperanto Society is buried, I imagine, a minute describing the terrible day Karinthy forgot Esperanto.

*   *   *

Looking through a book of "great moments in photo-journalism" published in the United States, I saw for the first time in years some of those photographs taken by Western journalists during the Hungarian Revolution, and was filled again with anger at the stupidity, or blind ambition, that allowed them to be published without masking the faces in the crowds. Many people were arrested and hanged because of those pictures.

In the same book there is one I had not seen before, of a frightened but very courageous young East German border guard lifting the barbed wire during the construction of the Berlin wall to let a child slip across into the West. If that soldier was not shot as a result of the photograph, he is certainly still behind bars. There is no doubt that whoever took the picture knew the magnitude of his or her crime, for the credit is anonymous.

Looking at things like this, one realizes again with a sinking heart that the prevailing philosophy of the West, sheer greed, is as revolting as the official philosophy of the East. It is hard to imagine the punishment suited to such a crime, and still harder to know what to think of a society that does not even know it is a crime.

June 20

While I was walking in the forest this morning, moving as silently as an Indian hunter on the soft carpet of moss and decaying foliage, two rather good lines occurred to me and I had to return home lest I forget them — there was everything in my canvas shoulder bag (nitroglycerin tablets, peppermints, passport, a bottle of ink) except my pen and notebook.

Someone once told me about a conversation at some international gathering between Paul Valéry and Albert Einstein. Valéry pulled a notebook from his pocket and wrote something in it, then, seeing Einstein's puzzled look, explained: "I always carry a notebook in case a good idea occurs to me. Don't you?" "I almost never have any good ideas," replied Einstein.

Neither have I, to say the least, but for many years have

carried the same battered notebook, bought in Buenos Aires in 1957, around the world with me, hoping. Flipping through it not long ago I noticed the following in E.'s hand in the blank pages near the end and remembered having asked him long ago in the restaurant of some German railway station who he thought the greatest benefactors of humanity were:

> Epicurus of Samos (for having discovered that the only problem of moral philosophy is happiness); Titus Lucretius Carus (for having made the doctrine of Epicurus available to Europe); William of Occam (for having shown that metaphysics do not exist); J. S. Bach (the voice of man rising to God), W. A. Mozart (the voice of God descending to man); François Marie Arouet de Voltaire (for having taught us better than the Church ever did that we have a conscience); the inventor of chloroform (for having given us the only wholly beneficial scientific discovery since the cooking fire); Ludwig Wittgenstein (for having, should anyone care to notice, demolished all the accumulated politico-metaphysical rubbish from Plato to V. I. Lenin).

June 21

Apart from the opprobrious labels applied to the artist by philistines in all ages ("eccentric," "dreamer," "Bohemian," etc.), an uncommon amount of high-flown cant has been written by philosophers and critics (and sometimes by artists themselves) in an attempt to distinguish art and its producers from the rest of humanity. I am tempted to make a small contribution.

It seems to me that what distinguishes the true artist from most others is what I think of as "creative anarchy." The artist, obviously, creates. Not so obviously, to the extent he really is an artist, he does so without so much as an unsatirical glance at the rules, assumptions, tastes, and prejudices of the prevailing middle-class humdrummery.

To go a bit further out on this limb, I shall suggest that there are among creative anarchists a left wing and a right wing. The right-wing anarchist is *committed*, though seldom to any point of view his neighbours would approve of. If he is political (like Bertolt Brecht, for example), he will be the despair of his party. If religious (like Tolstoy or Juan de la Cruz), he is likely to end up excommunicated or in the dungeons of the Inquisition.

But most artists are left-wing anarchists. Everything their neighbours hold as sacred—religion, family, money, the nation, and so on—is just so much grist for their mill. No other law is valid. Among poets Shakespeare is pre-eminently a left-wing anarchist, perhaps the high point in a tradition beginning with Sappho, continuing through Catullus, the Goliards and François Villon, and ending up in our own day in such figures as Lorca, Yeats, Esenin, Ady, Lörinc Szabó, and even, for all his Anglican posturing, W. H. Auden.

One might have thought that with the general collapse of our old bourgeois civilization the day of the left-wing anarchist would finally have arrived, but such is not the case. In a divided Germany, for instance, with the West believing in civilization no more than the East believes in revolution, a poet like Wolf Biermann is as much a voice in the wilderness as he would have been in the age of Goethe. And in North America a few very talented young poets either become minor establishment figures or, more often, wither on the vine. The situation is essentially as it always has been, with Athens, the T'ang Dynasty, and Lorenzo's Florence being the inexplicable exceptions that prove the rule.

All of which leads me to reaffirm a belief held since the age of sixteen: Bourgeois values actually have next to nothing to do with culture, the true voice of which, paradoxically, is always and everywhere the artist-anarchist who cocks a snoot at the prevailing superstitions and rit-

62

uals, who spends his days pissing against the wind and his nights whistling in the dark. That this point of view is now widely accepted as true is borne out by the incredible number of little magazines furiously engaged in both activities under the touching misapprehension that that is *all* there is to art.

*   *   *

Since my latest move to the Western world three decades ago, several short-lived eras of social concern have come and gone, brief flowerings of what I at first took for a new communal wisdom, but which soon revealed themselves as just so many popular fads. First there was the Cuban Revolution, then Détente, Civil Rights, the War in Vietnam, and finally the Environment—which has recently been losing ground to concern over South Africa. As far as I can see, there has been little essential, sustained popular interest in (let alone commitment to) any of these matters. Even the choice of issues defies rational explanation. I was reading recently that after the fall of Idi Amin the troops of his successor, Mr. Mbote, massacred an estimated 300,000 Ugandans. You can be sure no group in North America or West Europe ever protested that event, perpetrated as it was by blacks against blacks.

There seems in popular protest nowadays an assumption that the world's injustices are unconnected and can be solved piecemeal. That they have not been resolved in this fashion—indeed never really are—goes unnoticed. Most of those carrying anti-Apartheid signs this summer will be holding aloft quite different signs next year, their outrage, like their clothing and a lot of their vocabulary, having changed with the tide of fashion; and fashion, as Santayana points out, "produces innovation without reason and imitation without benefit." Being imitative *i.e.,* ape-like, it is a reminder of our simian past; and if in the matter of clothing it is merely silly, on the level of putative moral convictions it becomes revolting, for it casts serious doubt on what we assume, perhaps too hastily, to be the area of greatest advance from our branch-swinging past.

When next summer's marchers head down Yonge Street in Toronto, demanding justice for sea otters or lesbian mothers (or whatever will have captured their moral fancy by then), approach them with, say, an anti-Apartheid sign in your hand and just watch the reaction: the look of slightly puzzled amusement the *au courant* always accord the *passé*.

*   *   *

There is something ridiculous about our attitude towards time. People who would smile at the notion that Chilliwack, B.C., was the most important point in space do not hesitate to consider the point they themselves occupy in time the only one that really matters.

*   *   *

An odd, perhaps unique aspect of the age we're living in is what might be called "selective virtue." The idea of virtue— *areté, virtus, honestas*—has undergone many changes in three thousand years of Graeco-Roman and Judaeo-Christian civilization, but until now it was generally assumed to be one quality manifesting itself in various ways. Late 20th-century man, smiling at the moral earnestness of his Victorian grand-parents, has largely dismissed the notion of virtue as *vieux jeu*, but will often rather inconsistently single out some aspect of it as sort of personal adornment and be able to argue as subtly on its behalf as any mediaeval scholastic.

The motive for this is, I think, that while no longer believing in an overall propensity for goodness, modern man likes, as he often proclaims, to "feel good about himself," and finds it sufficient for this purpose to single out some congenial aspect of virtue and cultivate it in his spare time. Hence the woman (and sometimes the man) who argues knowledgeably about and campaigns fiercely against the evil of the "sexploitation" of women—who at the same time has no interest to speak of in any of the numerous other forms of exploitation, such as the permanent misery of those who have grown much of the food he or she eats, or that of the minimum wage-earners at the bottom echelons of his or her own business.

One of the most characteristic features of the mental life of the age in which we live is the way it has abandoned many of the inherited attitudes of our civilization and then, finding nothing with which to replace them, has ended up clinging for dear life to bits and pieces. Aristotle, no prude, would have more and better things to say against *Penthouse* magazine than the average feminist has ever dreamed of, for the simple reason that there's far more wrong with that publication than a one-track mind is ever likely to notice.

June 22

There were two squirrels on the cottage porch this morning waiting for me to give them their daily ration of peanuts. One ran to me, sat up, and made the same gesture the squirrels of Toronto always make, a little wave of one paw meaning, "Come on! Give!"

No poetry today. I took the day off, doing nothing but clean up the accumulated mess made by a hopelessly sloppy poet: egg yolk cemented to plates, cigarette ash under the desk, a black ring around the bathtub. All that done, I got rid of two huge plastic bags full of discarded drafts, notes, and assorted jottings, with only slight misgivings. It seemed the simplest solution.

The writer-in-exile, if a natural hoarder like myself, is faced with a problem: whom to hoard for? The National Library of Hungary has been asking me in recent years for old papers and MSS, but I have little inclination to give any official Hungarian institution (even that one) so much as the time of day. The National Archives in Ottawa several years ago gave me something called a "tax write-off" for some MSS, but as one had not earned enough to pay taxes in the first place it was not a useful gift. As I cannot imagine any of the institutions that reputedly pay huge sums for Dennis Lee's old laundry lists showing any interest in the random doodles of a poetic D.P. (some of which are scarcely legible even to their author), I've solved the problem by burning the lot. Anyway, *pace* Marshall McLuhan and the author of *Fahrenheit 451*, nothing counts, ultimately, except the printed page.

*   *   *

On the rare occasions I find myself outside Toronto and turned loose in the Canadian countryside, I always look around for arrowheads, stone axes, real evidence that there was someone here before John Cabot and I arrived. I know there was, but want tangible evidence. E. once found a coin from the reign of Alexander I while walking near Lake Ohrid, and on the beach in Tangier one day he suddenly stooped and picked up a little oil lamp washed smooth by centuries of waves and later identified as Carthaginian. I never find anything!

One likes to encourage archaeology, however, and when in Hungary at the end of the war I learned that the precious collections of the archaeological museum of Keszthely were being destroyed by leaking roofs and broken windows, I went up to the Minister of Finance and made a nuisance of myself until he handed me a bundle of money to take to them for repairs.

In those days the Social Democratic Party, not yet wiped out by the Communists, had given me a car and driver, a charming rogue named Alföldi who drove me all over the country to lecture to peasants, students, and anyone else who cared to be lectured to. I now told Alföldi to take me to Keszthely, and a few hours later I was banging on the door of the museum, which seems to be derelict. At last a suspicious curator peered out and I explained my mission.

Relieved that we weren't thieves or marauding Russians and overjoyed with the money, the man took us on a tour of the building, which housed some of the most precious finds, historical and prehistorical, in the country.

Afterwards, as Alföldi and I sat in a pub over glasses of wine, he smiled at me slyly and, contorting himself, pulled out from the back of his jacket the rusted but beautiful remains of a Bronze Age sword, the same one the curator had an hour earlier described as "the pride of the collection." "I though you might like it, Mr. Faludy," he said hopefully, anticipating my pleasure, and was a little hurt when I sighed and told him I would wait while he returned it. More perhaps than anyone else, it was Alföldi who taught me, if I had not known it before, that the relationship between essential goodness and the more ordinary virtues is not as close as people generally assume.

The last time I saw Alföldi was the day the Revolution broke out in October of 1956. My wife Zsuzsa and I were hurrying home on foot when suddenly a city bus going in the opposite direction screeched to a halt at the curb beside us, and Alföldi, the driver, leaned out. "Mr. Faludy!" he shouted. "Where are you going?" I told him, and as I did so he took Zsuzsa and myself by the arm and hustled us into the driver's compartment. Then, despite the furious protests of the passengers crammed in like sardines, he made a U-turn and drove us all the way to our doorstep, miles away in the wrong direction. By the time we got there, people had given up banging on the partition and were staring a little hatefully out the window as Alföldi kissed Zsuzsa's hand,shook mine, and then drove off into the Revolution and out of our lives forever.

June 23

I feel nothing but compassion (certainly no superiority!) for the millions past, present, and future who have been driven halfway or more around the bend by an existence in which pain, in the nature of things, must outweigh pleasure. If anyone doubts the truth of this latter assertion, Schopenhauer suggests that he "compare the feelings of an animal eating another one with those of the one being devoured." Despite reams of cant to the contrary, Anatole France's one-line history of the world remains sweepingly and irrefutably true: "They were born, they suffered, they died."

But—does one not take a certain *pleasure* in reading these bitter words? Even as one contemplates and acknowledges the sad truth of the human situation, hasn't a small, quite different possibility emerged to glimmer in the general darkness and remind us that even in hell the scenery may after all be beautiful or at least interesting? The pleasure we receive from watching a tragedy performed is not due to a feeling of relief that it's not happening to us. The joy inherent in the thing comes from the beauty that lurks potentially and paradoxically even in our calamities.

Once a man grasps that fact to the point of being able to apply it to his own life, the daily round begins to possess more entertainment than torment—"Except when he has a bad cold!" as an ancient scoffer said of the imperturbability of the Stoic sage. I am coming down with a bad cold, if not anything worse, and will abandon these ruminations in favour of bed.

June 25

Out of bed on shaky legs this morning, my temperature down, nose raw, sweat-soaked pajamas and bed linen soaking in a tub full of Tide and Javex.

After an almost equally severe washing of myself, followed by a lot of black tea, toast, and bacon, I went out onto the porch and was greeted by the cry of an enormous bird—quite obviously an eagle, though I hadn't known there were any here—sitting on a low branch of the largest tree before the cottage. As I watched, it opened wide its wings like the masthead of a legion standard and took off lazily with great flappings and a farewell screech in my direction. There was something Roman and auspicious about it, a friendly omen from an unknown god.

Life is constantly paying me these unexpected little dividends, as it always does the small investor who keeps his eyes open.

*　　*　　*

The worst of a bad cold, when you're over seventy, is that the thing can easily turn into pneumonia and carry you off at an irritatingly inconvenient moment. I sweated this one out under heaps of covers while amusing myself by mentally revisiting some of my favourite paintings. This usually means certain rooms in the Uffizi and the Vatican, but for some reason it was Rembrandt, Vermeer, and Avercamp who came into my mind yesterday: the greatest of portraits (Titus and Hendrickje) and the most wonderful of winter landscapes.

When I got up and sorted the mail, among the letters that had arrived was a tentative invitation to a future poetry festival in Rotterdam, where among those to be invited are Ted Hughes, Gary Geddes, Andrei Voznesensky, and my humble self. Now what, I wonder, is going on here? If I lie abed thinking about paintings, the ones that come to mind are, almost invariably, those of Michelangelo, Botticelli, Antonello da Messina. What caused me to revert suddenly to the 17th-century Dutch—and then to receive, hours later, an unexpected invitation to Holland?

June 26

Have received a letter from a man in Budapest who is a member of what Hungarians call the *Népiesek*. In English there is, happily, no real equivalent of that word. The chief characteristic of a *népies* is that all things Hungarian are the objects of his adoration and his chief reason for living. Though often a non-believer, he is ardently pro-Christian and always an anti-Semite to one degree or another (resembling in this his Soviet counterparts, the *Russity,* with whom Mr. Solzhenitsyn has so many affinities). The *népies,* in short, is something like a member of the John Birch Society or the White Guard who (if such a creature could be imagined) reads a lot of poetry and collects folk art.

Now in the minor cultures of Europe, of which Hungary is undeniably one, what has always separated the sheep from the goats is the extent to which one's mental furniture is European as opposed to merely local. All this fuss and passion focussed exclusively on the culture of a country with a population two-thirds that of Mexico City might seem to anyone who ever went beyond elementary school (and has a sense of humour and proportion) to be exaggerated. But the mark of a *népies* is not so much what he loves as what he hates: everything non-Hungarian within or near the borders of Hungary. Jews and Gypsies are definitely *Untermenschen* to him, and Slovaks of doubtful humanity. Like loonies everywhere, he is given to the writing of hate letters.

In this one I am accused, not for the first time, of being "amoral" in my poetry and, in any case, "not really a Hungarian poet." The only really disturbing thing in all three pages is the fact that he does not actually call my poetry bad—which leaves open the appalling possibility that the nut actually likes some of it, a thing to strike fear and self-doubt into the heart of any poet.

Thinking in broader terms and categories, as I try to do, patriotism of any really palpitating sort does not come naturally to me. But the letter from Budapest was well-timed, arriving as it does just before Canada Day. As long as the planet is divided into political entities, and as long as one has any choice among them, I rejoice with a shudder of incredulous delight that I've landed in this one where, as far as I know, no one has yet claimed that Irving Layton is not really a Canadian poet because he's a Jew, or Joyce Kogawa a Canadian writer because she's Japanese. God willing, it will stay that way *a mari usque ad mare.*

*   *   *

England has a long way to go to catch up with Canada in the matter of *népies* sentiment. My son Andrew, after suffering all his life from the stigma of having a foreign name in what is one of the most provincial societies in Europe, recently solved the problem by joining his own name to his wife's pristinely English one. My own helpful suggestion (rejected as "Not very funny, Dad") was that he change it to "McFaludy."

June 27

If you live most of your life as a wanderer and perpetual exile used to dealing with different customs, languages, and national characteristics, it becomes second nature to think of the world in terms of these multifarious divisions, which are interesting and real enough in their way but, in the long run, dangerously apt to shut out a larger truth. It is useful to be reminded, as I was today when reading Viktor Frankl's *Man's Search For Meaning,* that "there are two races of men in this world, but only these two—the 'race' of the decent man and the 'race' of the indecent man. Both are found everywhere; they penetrate into all groups of society. No group consists entirely of decent or indecent people."

June 28

E., who agrees with Umberto Eco that "there is nothing more wonderful than a list, instrument of wondrous hypotyposis," has sent me one of what he considers the world's most unjustly neglected books, several of which he has found in the antiquarian bookshops of Yugoslavia:

> In Beograd I turned up a Russian first edition of Arseniev's *Derzu the Hunter;* in Vinkovci, of all places, I found the original of Andrzejewski's *The Gates of Paradise (Bramy raju),* which Anthony Burgess praised twenty years ago and which, being first-rate but non-Soviet, has remained predictably unknown in the West. At the Tin Ujevich Antiquarian Bookshop in Zagreb I found the French original of Dumitriu's *Incognito*—a book so blatantly anti-Communist that it was a surprise to find it even in relaxed Yugoslavia. Marguerite Yourcenar is on sale in translation everywhere, as is Eco's *The Name of the Rose.*

Over the years, thanks to his passionate enthusiasms, I have come to know and sometimes love books previously ignored or too hastily cast aside: the works of George Santayana, for example, and on another level poets such as Wolf Biermann, Housman, Dylan Thomas, even the odd item by Edith Sitwell or Thomas Merton.

As for *The Name of the Rose,* which he loves with a tenderness having more perhaps to do with his own neo-mediaeval outlook than with literary quality, I have doubts about it—though it is, to say the least, a good read. In Canada I have met almost no one who really likes it, yet in Germany and Italy it is already a cult book. E.'s theories about its success may well be right: Its untranslated Latin is a delight for Europeans who spent their youths learning the language but who have not until now ever had any use for it; and it is, philosophically speaking, a sort of bridge between our own scholastic, believing past and the arid, rudderless present in which a knowledge of Latin is no longer required of an educated man (though we are never told what *is*). Finally it lovingly portrays an age during which it was still taken for granted that the universe was susceptible of explanation, a unified, logical whole, even if cracks were beginning to appear. It is a picture of the earliest days of our own time, the moment when the mediaeval mind was beginning to question itself, but without as yet any nihilism on the horizon, nor any of that metaphysical despair that lurks behind so much that is written and said today. Only in the final pages of Eco's book does all that creep tentatively in, when the protagonist, a disciple of William of Occam, turns the light of reason on God Himself and shudders at the void before his eyes.

"Yes, yes," mutter his sad spiritual descendants seven centuries later. I imagine an elderly retired professor of classics in a German (Italian, French, English, Hungarian) city, sitting in his attic and sighing at the end of *The Name of the Rose.* Downstairs his grandchildren (the first totally Latin-less and philosophy-less generation in European middle-class history) are listening to Pink Floyd from very loud stereo speakers. Beyond his dormer windows rise the spires of the local cathedral, still silently inviting one to a *Weltanschauung* difficult since the 18th century and by now all but impossible to accept. Our professor sighs and thinks, as nearly every generation of such men has thought in retirement: "This is the end of all that." This time, however, it appears to be true.

*   *   *

It seems some broadcasting company is bringing a week of live Soviet television to Canada via satellite, and in the article I am reading on the subject widely differing views are expressed. An M.P. of East European origins voices concern that ordinary Canadians will be defenceless against the propaganda and slanted view of Soviet life. A British television producer is quoted as saying that Soviet television, at its best, is superior to any other, whereas at its worst it is no more fatuous than most North American television. What all are agreed upon, apparently, is that state-controlled television is a bad thing, and that commercial television is intrinsically better because it is "free."

I myself am certainly no friend of state control over any medium, least of all my own, literature; but the arguments in favour of commercially controlled media leave me uneasy, to say the least. The assumption is that while political control is tyranny, control based on potential earnings is not; that the market place is the only just tribunal in these matters; and that being bound by its decisions is, somehow, freedom.

This is patently nonsensical. The dissident who can't get his play performed on Soviet television because it deviates from the party line is obviously the victim of tyranny; but so is the American playwright whose work is refused because, say, it takes a "risky" line in sexual (or conceivably even political) matters to the extent that no manufacturer of dishwashing liquid cares to sponsor it. The *area* of freedom is much greater in the West, but the difference is quantitative, not qualitative.

Having experience of both systems, I certainly prefer the tyranny of the market place—but only because its control over my affairs stops just there: in the market place. But it would be very naïve to assume that works are refused only on artistic grounds in the West, and only on political grounds in the East Block. And one would have to be a very great fool to assume that the powerful non-entities who rule over corporate North America have any more interest in such niceties as "artistic quality" than do the faceless dwarfs who line up on top of Lenin's tomb for May Day parades.

June 29

Various candidates are regularly proposed as the quality or faculty that separates us from the rest of the animal kingdom: speech, reason, etc. I submit that all these candidates might from a certain point of view be subsumed under the general heading of imagination. Imagination representing reality by symbols is called language. Imagination weeping over a sad novel is called sentiment. And imagination capturing and recording human experience in passionately distilled form is called art.

I don't know what to call that aspect of imagination at work in me today. I squandered five dollars on a frozen game bird, put it in the oven for two hours, until it was golden brown and sizzling in butter, and then, at the table, was utterly revolted by the sight of the little corpse with its feet amputated and its body curled up in the agony of death. Sighing, I took the thing out to the compost heap where some nocturnal creature, unhampered by the fantasy and reflection that make life on this planet so beautiful and so difficult for man, will devour it sooner or later.

These fits have come over me from time to time since the age of five or six. I am told that many children are natural vegetarians, refusing at first to eat meat once they learn its origins. This may be inconvenient for parents and the owners of slaughter houses, but it gives one hope for humanity, which, because it possesses imagination, can refuse to slaughter and devour its fellow creatures. Once in a while at least.

*   *   *

The newspaper has carried parts of a speech by Mr. Gorbachev in which he demands a return to socialist legality and morality. When I hear the latter phrase I always think of 1955 when my son Andrew was born. After I was released from prison by the so-called "post-Stalin thaw," my civil rights were not, of course, restored. Socialist legality may occasionally own up to having murdered and imprisoned on false charges, but the victim who survives it is still an "asocial element" (or what-not) and has no social insurance number.

My wife, always frail, her health further undermined by seven years of living in the workers' paradise, had not enough milk for the baby and so applied to the district committee for a ration of powdered milk. "I'm sorry," said the female comrade in charge. "As your husband has no social insurance number, you are not eligible." Suzy, desperate for our son, pleaded. "There is one possibility," said the woman at last. "If you are willing to state that Faludy is not the father, that the baby is illegitimate, we can give you an unwed mother's ration."

Eventually we got powdered milk through friends. Whenever Mr. Gorbachev or anyone else talks of a "return to socialist legality and morality," I remember that incident and sneer.

*   *   *

"The inherent vice of capitalism is the unequal sharing of blessings; the inherent virtue of socialism is the equal sharing of miseries."

— *Winston Churchill*

June 30

Trudging home from the store I was given a lift by a man whom I shall call Colonel Smedley-Smythe, Indian Army (Ret.). Smedley-Smythe lives several miles farther on and invited me to his cottage for lunch. He lived in a verandahed affair with a separate entrance for box wallahs. We sat in rattan chairs and ate large sandwiches washed down with gin and tonic. Mostly tonic in my case. He is about seventy, pink-faced, jolly, and about two hundred pounds of buoyantly British corporeality. He knows all there is to know about Vancouver Island and clearly regards it as a last outpost of Empire. Talking about the United States he waved his drink in the direction of Washington state, which he seems to regard as a sort of Kafiristan, full of vaguely threatening lesser breeds without the law.

What I like about this type of anachronistic Englishman is

the rock-bottom humanity, good sense, and humour that generally lurks just beneath the mannered surface. At one time, after watching Alec Guinness building the bridge over the River Kwai, I had thought the type an invention of the film industry. But then I met a colonel who had actually been there—George Sully of Ready Money Cove, Cornwall, who with his wife, Jane, once lent me a house during a homeless period—and I realized that the species really exists and that the world is the better for it.

After lunch today I was given an extraordinarily good Yunnan tea, then driven home with *panache*. If the Kafirs ever do invade, I'll be proud to stand beside Smedley-Smythe in the trenches. Hungarian poets have come to worse ends.

*   *   *

One is, of course, aware of the less pleasant aspects of British life: a tendency towards petty malice, sniffy hauteur, and some of the sillier varieties of snobbery, including minute classification of accent from Clapham Junction subliterate to High Church whinnying. And then there's the Question of Sex. Even after I had become a British subject, the national sexual neurosis continued to baffle me. One could only note that the Continental saying was probably true: England is a country where the milk on your front porch will remain untouched but your child not.

A not terribly revealing sidelight was shed on the Question of Sex when my wife and I rented a room in our Mill Hill house to a nondescript but mild-mannered young man who was dubbed "Donald the Duck" by my young son Andrew. Donald, as thin walls soon revealed to us, was in the habit of bringing home partners of both sexes. Being neither petits bourgeois nor regular readers of St. Paul, we were broad-minded and tried to give him (them) as much privacy as possible.

One night, however, I got out of bed to look in on Andrew, who had the flu, and while I was in his room, I heard Donald coming up the stairs panting drunken endearments, "Jimmy, you gorgeous creature, just wait until I get you into bed!" and the like. I was standing in the dark beside Andrew's bed out of sight and, being curious, I watched as Donald passed by the open door. He was *alone*.

I've always been grateful to England for having taken us in after 1956, and I am a life-long admirer of the British Way of Life. But all in all, I'm rather relieved not to live there anymore.

*   *   *

My Toronto physician, Stephen Lazarovits, has sent me a book called *Peter's Quotations* in which four entries are attributed to me, though I cannot remember ever having uttered three of them and cannot now imagine what I meant by the fourth. The following, by others, are included under the heading "Poetry":

> "Publishing a volume of verse is like dropping a rose petal down the Grand Canyon and waiting for the echo." —Don Marquis
> "If it makes my whole body so cold no fire can warm me, I know that is poetry." — Emily Dickinson
> "He does not write at all whose poems no man reads." — Martial
> "Poets are born, not paid." — William Mizner

*   *   *

People have sometimes surprised me by saying they wished themselves as happy as I appear to be. Be that as it may, the amount of intense unhappiness one notes on every side has never ceased to shock and dismay me. Happiness is, as Aristotle says, the only thing we desire for its own sake. That presumably makes it, whatever the metaphysicians may say, the *summum bonum*. Santayana, with his usual lucidity, says that nothing else in fact justifies human existence: "Where happiness fails life remains a mad and lamentable experiment."

Can anyone say of himself that he is happy? I myself enjoy life, and savour its small pleasures and joys as far as possible, whether in an idyllic cottage in the woods or in a concentration camp. Asking a cheerful man why he's so happy is like asking a nonagenarian the secret of his longevity. He doesn't really know. If cornered, however, I would hazard this much: Happiness seems to me to be grounded in vital activity, either mental or physical. It's very hard to be depressed while digging a garden or writing a poem: Both activities make the blood flow fresh and clean and give the mind no time for pointless and sickly thoughts of what was, might have been, or will be. To crawl out still further on a shaky limb I'll even hazard this thought: Happiness is living solidly in the present reality while regarding it with some of the indulgence people usually reserve for fiction.

Most unhappiness seems to me to come from a kind of disordered contemplation of things. If one looks and listens to things as they are, depriving them of their usual load of adventitious significance, they reveal themselves to us without venom. Art and nature furnish some of the most intense joys known to man, but lamentably few people manage to contemplate either without injecting some poison of their own into the experience, thus rendering it bitter, desperate, and Romantic. Though it is obviously abnormal, I must suppose that happiness is, simply and paradoxically, sanity.

*   *   *

July 1

And now it is July. In Hungary, hordes of hopeful holiday-makers will be heading for Lake Balaton, exchanging over-crowded apartments for inadequate little tents. It is pleasant to watch some nations (the Italians, the Yugoslavs, the Chinese, for example) enjoying themselves. Others, attempting the same end, can be a depressing sight: one thinks of the English at the seaside, German tourists truffling their way around Spain, Hungarians whooping it up.

Insofar as Hungary has any reputation at all in the world, it is, I suppose, for a certain semi-Balkan *joie de vivre:* Gypsy music, operetta manners, the boot-stomping *csár- dás,* and corks popping in the wee hours of the morning. The truth, alas, is that my countrymen often have a lot standing between themselves and even a quite ordinary enjoyment of life: an almost unbelievable lust for gain that is working much of the male population to heart failure and an early grave; a tendency to look for the main chance to the exclusion of all else; a mildly but persistently oppressive State Security Police; and the world's highest suicide rate. Thirty out of every hundred thousand Hungarians kill themselves each year, as opposed to (roughly) thirteen Canadians or Scandinavians.

In my periods of exile—well over half my life now—I have seldom encountered anyone among my fellow emigrés with whom it was possible to discuss any of these grimmer aspects of Hungarian life and character seriously. Self-analysis is not a Magyar strong point, and reflection in general seems to exert little appeal. Perhaps that is why the country has never produced a major philosopher and fewer minor ones than Denmark or Spain.

Perhaps this reluctance to reflect deeply is a defence mechanism, like the national penchant for turning catastrophies into anecdotes. And perhaps that is why, at three in the morning—with the wine still flowing and exhausted Gypsies still churning out those dreary melodies with embarrassing lyrics about the colour of roses—the faces around one always wore the grey aspect of spiritual exhaustion, of not knowing what hit them and having no real desire to find out.

In the meantime it is drizzling and misting in that curiously un-North American way that makes British Columbia look some days like a landscape by Sesshu. If anyone is attempting to put up a tent at the site down the road, they must be pretty miserable. But Camper's Haven is not Lake Balaton, and no one is very likely to hang himself in despair.

*   *   *

The first more-or-less forced emigration of Hungarian dissidents in modern times occurred in 1849, after the failure of the uprising against the Habsburgs. The second, incomparably greater one, occurred in 1956-57, after the failure of the revolt against the Russians and their puppet government in Budapest.

I wonder if the first occasion was not more painful for an ardent lover of his native land, "the feather in God's cap," as the jingoistic song has it. In 1849 the relationship of Hungary with Western civilization was rather more tenuous than it now is, and one is not surprised to find that many of the exiles preferred Constantinople to Paris.

Thing have changed. Those who left in 1956 were, in most senses, Europeans, and the old saying *Extra Hungariam non est vita* would have struck them as slightly silly. Even more so today among the young people who are trickling out. One such person recently spent some weeks in my living room, finding his feet in Canada with extraordinary speed—the interests, music, and conversation of his generation in Canada are much the same now as in Hungary or almost anywhere else. He was more comfortably at home in five weeks than I myself had been after five years.

There are moments, *very* occasionally, when I have looked out of my window in Toronto at the acres of concrete that form the entire horizon and have felt a twinge of nostalgia for a Hungary that used to be. *Estne vita extra Hungariam?* Indeed there is, and surrounded as one is in Toronto by Hungarian food, newspapers, and other things that sometimes make it seem like a suburb of Budapest, there are days when one regrets not having got farther away, to Goose Bay for instance.

*   *   *

Statistics from the well-named (in this instance) StatsCan: Canadians produce fifty million kilos of garbage daily, over two kilos for every inhabitant. Looking with some astonishment at the vast amount of rubbish I myself have already added to the compost heap behind the cottage, I can well believe it.

*   *   *

Felt a strong stab from my "silent" kidney stones while writing this afternoon, and sternly addressed the various organs of my body, a little habit of mine for some years now, reminding them that the watchword is not *sauve qui peut* but *one for all and all for one.* When anyone mutinies, we'll all be done for.

July 3

Today is the 168th birthday of Mr. Edward Rehatsek, and there are probably only two people in the world who have noted the fact: myself, in this cottage, and E., who (as he writes) has been wading through the monsoon-flooded streets of Bombay trying to locate the unpublished manuscripts Rehatsek deposited with the "Native General Library" at the time of his death in 1892.

He was the son of a Hungarian forest inspector, and after those humble beginnings took a degree in civil engineering in Pest and emigrated to the United States. In 1847 he left New Orleans, sailed to Bombay, and settled there for the rest of his life. He seems to have supported himself in a variety of ways in British India, but ended up teaching at Wilson College. Apart from his native Hungarian and Croat, he knew, *really* knew, German, Arabic, Persian, French, Latin, Gujurati, and English. In the catalogues of very major libraries, his name appears only as the translator of Saadi's *Gulistan*, a Persian classic. It is in my opinion, as in that of others better qualified to judge, the best translation of the work in any European language and by far the best of the many versions in English. When not learning languages Rehatsek wrote voluminously on many themes and was often visited in his tumble-down little house in the native quarter of Bombay by the likes of Sir Richard Burton and other bearded luminaries of the Royal Geographic Society come to pick his brain. When he died at the age of seventy-two, he left thirty-thousand rupees "for the education of poor Indian boys," all saved from his years of teaching and ascetic living. His was the first European body to be cremated Indian-style.

Rehatsek was one of several Hungarians who wandered the East. The best known are probably Alexander Csoma de Koeroes and Arminius Vámbéry. Csoma de Koeroes spent years in a tiny room in Tibet compiling the first scholarly grammar and lexicon of the language. Arminius Vámbéry (the father of my great friend and mentor Rustem Vámbéry, familiar to readers of *My Happy Days in Hell*) was the self-educated, crippled son of a Jewish tailor who rose to such fame as a traveller and scholar that Rustem was actually born during a family visit to Windsor Castle. Rehatsek lived and died, by comparison, in total obscurity. Except for a small number of scholarly articles, nothing is known of the rest of his work except that he wrote it. My Hungarian encyclopaedia is unaware of his existence, and so is the Hungarian Academy of Sciences, to which E. wrote some time ago. He writes to me now from Bombay that having followed up various clues from academics and librarians, he is on the point of giving up the search:

> Rehatsek's papers, if they have survived the climate at all, are probably buried in one of those Indian archives where bundles of documents tower to the ceiling until devoured by mice and fungus. At the University not even the oldest scholar (nearly a hundred years old, they told me) had so much as heard of my Hungarian or of a "Native General Library." So I have now given

up looking for the remains of that perhaps mythical institution, but have in the meantime found some wonderful books, locally printed editions of all sorts of things including, *rarissima avis,* a Ladakhi grammar.

"Bombay is afloat in water and muck. As I cannot afford many taxis and hate rickshaws, I splash everywhere in rubber thongs. Yesterday, trying to track down the site of R.'s house in Khetwady, I lost both thongs in the middle of the flooded street, then trying to retrieve them, dropped and lost forever an illustrated edition of *The Birds of Garhwal and Tehri.* Am by now desperately eager to get out of this wretched city, and will travel tonight back to Delhi and then on to the hill country north of Dehra Doon to walk through the clouds with real shoes on my feet."

*   *   *

Came across an essay tonight by Kingsley Amis in which he gives one of those lists of "the world's shortest books," beginning with *Great Marxist Humanitarians* and *Canadian Wit and Humour*—comfortably malicious, academic, sherry-flavoured British humour. As I not long ago read part of one of Mr. Amis's own novels, I venture to add a third title to his list: *Enduring Classics of Contemporary British Fiction.*

*   *   *

It is a curious comment on our own civilization that when anyone tells us of some distant paradise—usually tropical and insular—the first thing we ask is: "Has it been spoiled yet?" and we mean by that: "Have *we* got there yet?"

July 4

Bright sunshine today, though there is never enough here to dry things completely. I found a cane in a bedroom closet and borrowed it to stroll down the road with that fine sense a walking stick always gives one of possessing whatever it lands on. Then a few lightning-like stabs of sciatica warned me I had gone far enough. Apart from having seen almost everything at least once, the worst of growing old is not being able to dash about finding things one has *not* seen.

The year I entered the world as one of his subjects, the Emperor Franz Josef was still firmly on the throne of Austria-Hungary. Tolstoy died that year, as did Koch, and Swinburne had died the year before. Still alive were the Empress Eugénie (widow of Napoleon III), Lord Kitchener, Claude Debussy, Sarah Bernhardt and Henry James. Adolf Hitler was a starveling street artist in Vienna that year, Lawrence of Arabia a student at Oxford, Sergei Esenin a fifteen year-old peasant lad in central Russia; and in Zürich an obscure crank named Vladimir Lenin was thinking (happy thought!) of emigrating to America and going into business.

But nothing makes me feel quite so ancient as a memory from my ninth or tenth year, when my parents took me to Paris. Walking with us near the Opéra, a French chemist, a colleague of my father's, pointed out a gentlemen in a top hat as Anatole France, the favourite author of my childhood, born (I think) around 1844 and still going strong.

*   *   *

A letter from New Delhi:

> The centre of this town, from the tourist's point of view, is Connaught Circle, over a mile in radius, lined with rotting two-storey columns and alive all day long with the endless, screeching roar of aged vehicles speeding around it as around one of the lower circles of hell, going nowhere.It's the Third World in microcosm. Walking here and there this morning I found myself in a quiet area of trees and villas, and stopped a long time to watch a family of mongooses coming and going through a hole in a garden wall.

The book stores of New Delhi are not so good as those of Zagreb, but much better than Toronto's. There is a great hunger for knowledge here, and one finds ragged youths selling heaps of pirated books on the pavement and able to discuss their wares quite knowledgeably. Outside the Bank of Japan I stopped to talk to a motor-rickshaw driver who was reading a Penguin edition of Jan Morris's *The Matter of Wales*. He had paid twenty rupees for it—two days' wages, he said. Moved, I had him drive me back to my hotel and there gave him two more Penguins plus five rupees for the fare. I am permanently exhausted and emotionally drained by this country, by its heat and dirt, its abysmal poverty beside ostentatious wealth, by stupidity side by side with bright-eyed intelligence.

This evening I walked to Nerula's, a complex of first-class hotel, Chinese restaurant, and fast-food bar, suddenly hankering for something familiar to eat. All the gilded youth of Delhi gather there for ten-rupee ice-cream cones and the like. After two chocolate milk shakes, I left and almost stumbled on the pavement over a woman lying on a rag, hugging an infant to her breast. Standing up with the baby she smiled and held out a small garland of white flowers she had strung together but had not managed to sell during the day. She certainly caught me at the right moment, and as a result both of them will eat for at least the next two weeks.

This afternoon I took a motor-rickshaw a short distance, as I was lost in what looked like a red-light district. The driver, a Sikh, turned back and asked me if I would like a "nice, clean girl." I glanced at the scabrous buildings on either side of the road and the garbage piled high in the gutters and must have had an odd expression on my face, for he began to laugh, then suddenly we were both laughing together.

There also came today a letter from a friend at the University of British Columbia who, mentioning E.'s wanderings, writes: "He's one of those passionate scholars who would walk farther for a footnote than most of us would drive for a book."

*   *   *

A friend writes that a professor at the University of Toronto is publishing a book on something called "Hungarian-Canadian literature" in which I am not very favourably compared with certain other exiled writers, apparently on the grounds that I have never "gone home" to recharge my linguistic batteries on the agitprop of the press and the current slang of the toiling masses.

The idea that there is such a thing as a Hungarian-Canadian literature is, to say the least, open to debate. On the one hand, it smacks of a literary hegemony that Anglo-Saxons clearly cannot claim; on the other, it lumps together for purposes of ethnographical convenience three or four genuine writers with a lot of dilettantes and versifiers. Brecht, Mann, and even poor Franz Werfel were never "German-American" writers any more than Malcolm Lowry or D. H. Lawrence were Anglo-Mexicans. The whole business is too silly for words, but, as the great Franco-New England novelist Maggie Yourcenar put it, *"On est toujours pris au piège avec ces gens."*

The truth is that almost every Hungarian with a pen in his hand is a "poet," and every untenured academic hack, lest he perish, must, notoriously, publish. But (I remind myself) it doesn't do to attack the witless and soon-to-be-forgotten too harshly. The Budapest papers complain that smuggled volumes of my poetry change hands for substantial sums of money in Hungary nowadays. One smiles at the stratagems a man would have to employ to unload a history of Hungarian-Canadian literature anywhere at any price. And laughter, as V. Nabokov (the popular Russo-Swiss writer who died at Montreux a few years ago) once noted, is the best pesticide.

July 5

Sitting at the kitchen table this evening as a large moth made *kamikaze* attacks on the lamp, I read Wolfgang Hildesheimer's new Mozart biography, an extremely interesting, acerbic document that leaves one convinced, if one wasn't already, of the ineffable silliness of most other biographers of Mozart, of the impossibility of knowing what he or anyone else before the French Revolution was really like, least of all that strange, lubricious young man who may well have been the "greatest genius of all time."

It's a sometimes repetitious book, but filled with unexpected insights: "Self-reflection, for the genius, is not a general subject; but for the would-be genius, it is not only subject matter but an instrument. He plays the role of genius and demands tribute as such, calculating all the while how to integrate unproductiveness into his thematic program." Hildesheimer then goes on rather savagely on the theme of Rilke as would-be genius.

Well, Wolfgang, yes and no. In the 1930s, my salad days, strutting around Budapest in English suits and sporting a monocle on occasion (which awful fact I cannot now forget as Corgi Books has recently used photographic evidence of my affectation on the cover of my autobiography), like nearly everybody else I adored Rilke. The first doubts arose when Dezsö Kosztolányi, an extremely fine poet, told me that anyone with any imagination at all could improvise convincing Rilkean verses in a coffeehouse. To prove it, he drained his cup and began spouting lines that sounded extraordinarily like the sonnets to Orpheus—but were in fact sonorous twaddle about emotions and gods. Made thoughtful, I reserved judgment until some years later it became clear that Kosztolányi was right.

There is more to Rilke than that, however. With the notorious and almost incredible exception of Baudelaire, I do not believe that any poet of the past hundred years has more than ten poems carved in gold in the *museion* atop

Parnassus. Four or five indisputably permanent master-pieces (Yeats, Lorca, Esenin) are a lot; two or three (Graves, Auden, Frost, Cavafy, Pasternak, Georgi Ivanov, Attila József, Lörinc Szabó, Endre Ady) place one among the giants; and even one is a guarantee of immortality, so rare in this world is the real thing.

It is that one that causes real poets (as opposed to bunglers, who are always certain of their greatness) to look anxiously at their own collected works sometimes and tremble. In his "Torso of an Archaic Apollo", Rilke has written, at the very least, that one. Personally I should say he has at least three, none of them from his Orphic period.

I think Hildesheimer has been misled by the fact that Rilke is supremely good about as often as Mozart is genuinely bad. He misses the point that all it takes is *one*. No amount of self-analyzing, self-indulgent rubbish will ever outweigh that single gem—so long as one has produced it.

*   *   *

Some awesome moments in world literature:

The court ladies' outing in *The Pillow Book of Sei Shonagon*, when a spray of wisteria is caught in the spokes of the carriage and is carried past the window again and again.

The recognition scene in Thomas Mann's *The Holy Sinner,* when the hero Grigorss and his lover, Sybilla, simultaneously discover that she is not only his mother but (owing to still earlier incest) his aunt, and that Herrad, their daughter, is thus at once Sybilla's daughter and granddaughter.

Alyosha Karamazov at the deathbed of Captain Snegirev's son, Ilyusha.

Euripides' Elektra, realizing that the visitor to the hovel she lives in is her lost royal brother, Orestes.

The death of Antinoüs in Yourcenar's *Memoirs of Hadrian.*

The transformation of the nun in Isak Dinesen's *The Monkey.*

July 6

Every human being has known great suffering, and nearly everybody, at one time or another, great joy. I wonder why both play such a small role in one's present consciousness. Women are said to forget the pains of childbirth, and no one winces remembering a painful tooth-extraction of thirty years before; nor does anyone flush with genuinely recaptured pleasure remembering the rapture of a youthful romance. Epicurus seems to be wrong when he suggests (or rather insists: Epicurus never *suggests* anything) that a large part of present happiness is the memory of past bliss. On the contrary, it is more likely to be the occasion of mild melancholy.

Real melancholy, the sort one sometimes wakes up with for no apparent reason, as I did this morning, an overpowering sense of emptiness and futility, is in my experience certainly not to be cured by any contemplation of past joys, but by the cultivation of small present tasks and pleasures: the reading (or better, writing) of a poem, the creation and/or contemplation of something on the human scale, the only scale that really suits us.

I doubt that it is wonder, as the ancients claimed, that gives rise to philosophy, at least to that branch we call metaphysics: It is fear and melancholy in the face of a cold and unknowable universe in which, in our present individual forms, we are temporary visitors. My own remedy—the one everybody's Aunt Tilly would tritely and rightly have recommended—is to turn the offending faculty, the imagination, in the direction of the warm, agreeable and knowable. To write a poem, to read a story attentively, to weed a garden, is to domesticate the universe for the moment— and the present moment, after all, is the only one we ever live in.

Il faut cultiver notre jardin. When Votaire put that immortal phrase in the mouth of Candide, he said something essentially happy people have always known instinctively, something Plato never found out. One of the major crimes our civilization has committed in the process of lifting *Homo europaensis* out of poverty is to have taken him so far from anything resembling a garden and to have made him largely passive in his pleasures, and so almost incapable of joy.

This cottage and garden are not going to be mine very long now. Coming to my senses, I clipped the hedge as enthusiastically as creaky joints would allow and observed my own melancholy wryly. It always works. A passion observed, as Spinoza says somewhere, ceases to be a passion. Melancholy, like lust, has to be cultivated. Hedge-clippers, vigorously wielded, nip such things in the bud.

*   *   *

Flipping down the dial of the radio, I heard someone announce that the lady who had just sung was named Streisand. I wonder how many North Americans know the origins of that and similarly sad Jewish names. They are yet another product of the fabled land of my birth, The Austro-Hungarian Empire. It seems that under Josef II it was decided that everyone had to have a family name. As many *shtetl* Jews did not, local officials awarded them such names as Greenspan (the poison that forms on a silver spoon left in the mayonnaise), Goldfarb (gold colour), Streisand (the sand strewn to dry ink), and, most insulting of all, Ostertag (Easter Day).

It ought to be said, however, that the Empire was a comparative liberal haven in the sickening history of Christian-Jewish relations. For a certain amount of money the officials could be persuaded to bestow marginally less offensive names, those of animals for example. Hence the multitude of Wolffs, Katzes, and Vogels scattered around the world. All these names are enduring monuments to the depths of vicious stupidity and vulgarity Christian Europe has so often descended to.

July 7

A long, reminiscing letter today from an old friend, a professor of philosophy in New York, describing his efforts as a soldier in the U.S. Army of Occupation to obtain a degree at Heidelberg shortly after the war. His thesis was rejected on the grounds that it was written in English, which was not a *Kultursprache*, a "language of civilization." No great fan of *Deutsche Kultur*, I had to laugh reading about this piece of spirited insolence and defiance of authority—though an attitude that would have been useful in the Germany of 1937 was, in 1947, merely amusing.

In the meantime English has, whatever German professors may think of it, come into its own with a vengeance. It is the *Kultursprache par excellence* and has become the international *lingua franca*, though one regrets that some lesser medium, such as Lapp or Swahili, has not been conscripted for that use. When French was the international language, many crimes were committed against it, but French, being academically ossified and insulated, is comparatively immune to misuse, and suffered little compared to the universal slaughter of English, a language infinitely harder to learn with real fluency than any purely Romance language.

Be that as it may, English remains not only the one truly universal literary language ever to have swept the entire planet, but is also the tongue richest in vocabulary, fluidity of syntax, and superabundance of literary and historical association, nuance, etc. It also has an ability to adapt that has caused many other languages to disappear altogether. Unlike French (furiously and fatuously trying to rid itself of *le weekend* and *le parking*), English has an insatiable appetite for loan-words.

As far as I can see, the only thing threatening it is its very universality. Very few foreigners (as I know from long and bitter personal experience) ever learn to handle English as it deserves to be handled. To teach it rather than some lesser Esperanto in schools from Tokyo to Buenos Aires is to give beginners a Stradivarius to practise on. No one should be surprised if the results set the teeth on edge.

The situation does not look as if it were changing, and in one sense at least there is a sort of wry justice in this universal sparrowdom of what is (or until recently was) the noblest of living languages. Such *Kultur* as our age possesses is pre-eminently Contemporary Anglo-Saxon, *i.e.*, it is technocratic, money-minded, and power oriented. In its manners and artifacts, it is recognizably American right down to the grey flannel uniforms and suburban cultural attitudes in the corridors of power everywhere. Russian and Japanese culture stand no chance whatsoever against it, a fact reflected in the statistics concerning whose children are learning what language.

No, if you are anyone at all in these last years of the 20th century, if you are affluent, well-travelled, and at least half-educated, English will be your second language if it's not already your first. Travel to Hamburg, for instance, and you will hear it at the airport, at the check-in counter, in the restaurant, and in the hotel lobby, often in conversations better couched in Pidgin or Volapük:

"Well then, Monsieur Spelican," says Herr Geldmacher (likewise dressed by Saville Row, the Via Veneto and Beverly Hills). "I tink ve are agreet: de grenades vill go via Dar es Salaam und de anti-tank rockets via Addis Ababa. Shall ve haf a drink on dis in de bar?"

"Unfortunately," replies M. Spelican, glancing at his platinum Rolex, "I must to go now. My wife is waiting and we are coming at ze opera tonight."

"So?" says Geldmacher, a glint of amused linguistic superiority in his eyes. "What plays tonight?"

"Tonight one plays *Carmen*."

"Ah, my favourite Spanish opera. Vell, goodbye, my frent. Abyssinia again soon, I hope."

A plague, say I—albeit in the thickest of accents—on both their houses.

*   *   *

A German magazine, hidden among the *Time* collection in the bathroom, gives statistics on the standard of living of various countries, based on the large assumption that the number of cars, TV sets, and radios per person has something fundamental to do with it.

I would propose another method of divining which countries are fit (and fun) to live in and which ought to be fled even at the risk of life and limb. I suggest that if a country scores less than five out of the following ten considerations, the inhabitants would do well to drop whatever they are doing and run for the border:

1) Freedom to leave without an exit visa or baggage search is assumed;
2) Faces of the population are generally cheerful;
3) Public rudeness is rare;
4) Fairly elaborate manners are expected of everyone after the age of seven
5) Public libraries are uncensored, well-stocked, and much-used;
6) Little or no hunger or squalor is evident, though the accumulation of wealth is not generally thought of as the Meaning of Life;
7) Violence is rare and, among the police, *severely* forbidden;
8) A general attitude is live and let live;
9) No political prisoners are taken;
10) Few are destitute and those few are charitably treated.

It will be seen at once that a few countries (Iceland, Denmark, Canada) come off reasonably well, with others (Tunisia, Costa Rica, France, the United States, etc.) hovering somewhere in the middle ground. At the bottom, as on anybody's scale, will be such nightmares as Uganda, Albania, Cambodia, Honduras, etc.

*   *   *

I do not know what creates civilization, but suspect strongly that what keeps it in existence is nothing more than an unrelenting preference for the agreeable on the part of the few in the face of wide-spread opposition.

July 8

A Hungarian religious periodical, tolerated by the State, has a long and unintentionally funny article against astrology and other superstitions—it defines religion as worship of the divine, superstition as an attempt to *use* it. The author has apparently forgotten Lourdes, Fatima, and prayers to St. Anthony. Actually the piece might just as well have been printed by a Communist publication, because whatever Marxism may say about its antagonism to superstition, its real reasons are the same as those of the Church: Neither likes the idea of any influence other than its own holding sway over the human imagination. I have no use for superstition myself (including Marxism, astrology, and dogmatic theology), but am reminded of at least one occasion when it saved me from coming to grief. This was in Tangier in 1978. I told the little story only once in Toronto, and saw incredulity written on the faces across the table. Anyone who has ever lived in Morocco will recognize it as nothing very unusual.

There is, or used to be, an open-air coffeehouse just outside Tangier on a hillside overlooking the Atlantic. Finishing my mint tea one afternoon, I walked beyond the café along a rather narrow path, foolishly going on even when the path became nothing more than a ledge on the side of a cliff. But the real danger, as I discovered when at last I turned around, was a young Arab following me about ten feet behind, barefoot, a slight smile curling his lips, and a broken bottle half raised in his hand.

"*Flus!*" he said, coming closer. One part of my mind told me I had better obey; a more intelligent part, knowing I might well end up on the rocks below whether I gave him my money or not, grew angry and suggested a better idea.

Forcing a look of amusement on my face, I began to laugh. If you can get one convincing laugh out under such circumstances, you can produce more. I did so, and slowly slid to a sitting position, my back against the cliff, as if overcome by mirth. Wiping imaginary tears from my eyes, I looked at him with largely unfeigned disdain.

"Why you laugh?" he demanded uneasily in English. (Frenchmen, he knew, didn't behave that way.)

"*Petit idiot,*" said I, "don't you know that I am a *djinn* and the son of *djinns*? What do you want to become? A dog? A snake? Or would you rather I hurled you off the cliff?" Laughing again, even harder, I got up and took a step towards him with a vicious smile. He backed up, nearly missing his footing on the ledge.

"*Sois prudent, petit idiot. Si tu crèves, c'est moi qui l'arrangerai!*" I was about to say more, but he suddenly threw the bottle into the sea, turned, and fled as fast as he could manage on the dangerous path. I sat awhile on the ledge, then slowly walked back past the café and on towards home, feeling rather older than usual.

I mentioned the incident some days later at a gathering of old *Tangerois*, and all nodded in grim recognition, recollecting similar scenes in their own lives. Only my hostess, a French lady preoccupied with all things occult—her "astral body" journeyed to Tibet several times a year to consult with certain Masters—took me aside and said with great delight: "I knew it! There was always something about you that told me so! But, you're such a kind man, George. You wouldn't really have turned him into a snake, would you?"

*   *   *

On the radio this afternoon there was an hour of strange eerie music—rather beautiful to me, who am no judge—which the announcer said was Heian Court music of 11th-century Kyoto. So much on Vancouver Island proclaims that this landscape is the other shore of a pool bounded on the West (as it were) by Japan. I regret now that I never visited that country when it was still recognizable as its historical self, that the only time I saw it was during the last days of the war when, during my brief and unheroic career as a tail-gunner, Tokyo moved beneath my plane, a flattened, smoking ruin.

In its literature, in its architecture, even in its unfathomable music, Japan has exerted an attraction only an aesthetic imbecile could entirely resist. But at the same time there is something repellent in its culture, an air of underlying violence, hysteria, even insanity. It's too late for me to unravel that mystery for myself now. The air fare alone is impossibly high, and by all accounts the Japan that fascinates me is long gone.

Many years ago, when for some reason I was invited to a gathering of British cognoscenti—literary lions and Bloomsbury remnants—I found myself in a corner talking with a member of the Sitwell family who, *apropos* nothing (perhaps my mere foreignness, abroad being "all the same"), began telling me that if he could choose any historical time and place to live in it would be the Heian Court of Murasaki Shikibu. Some years later, at breakfast on a rooftop overlooking Tangier in the summer of 1974, Ivan Morris, perhaps the greatest Japanese scholar of his generation, made the same unexpected remark to me.

My own choice would be quite different: I would be court poet to Lorenzo the Magnificent, and with any luck at all a very successful one, as the poets around Lorenzo were all pretty bad! When not scribbling verses in the gardens at Carreggi I would haunt the tiny streets and disreputable dens around the Bargello. Passing obliquely allusive, exquisitely penned poems around the court of the Prince Genji is not my idea of paradise.

Still, sitting here among damp ferns and ancient twisted trees, with the echo of that Heian music still hanging like perfume in the air, one feels unimaginably far from Florence and quite close to Asia. The harshness of Canadian nature is softened here: Mist rises, the splash of a frog in the pond takes on haiku-like significance. Vancouver Island is a floating world, though it too is tragically disappearing under the chainsaw and, like Japan, the cult of big bucks. In the meantime

> "I often smile, admonishing my humble self not to sorrow unnecessarily."
>
> — *Lu Yu, 1125-1209 A.D.*

*   *   *

J. G. Ballard's *Empire of the Sun* which I came across last year and perused again recently, is perhaps the second-best portrait known to me of that other side of Japanese civilization, the moon-struck cult of violence, pain, and death. The best picture, I think, is given by Laurens van der Post. Ballard's book, besides being beautifully written and intensely moving, is a reminder that nothing in this life is simple. Sadism is as normal among us as kindness. Like Van der Post, however, he refuses to sit in judgement, no doubt remembering, as we all ought to, that moral condemnations don't carry much weight coming from the contemporaries of Auschwitz, Dresden, Kolima, and the South Bronx.

July 10

Walking in the drizzle today, I found myself thinking of Talian for the first time in years. Talian was a fellow prisoner of mine in Recsk, though he was a *capo*, an overseer who informed on and regularly tortured the rest of us—especially me, because I gave lectures at night to my comrades. It was said that Talian had been a smuggler of refugees across the border into Austria, but instead of leading his clients to safety he had pocketed their money and disposed of them quite otherwise. Being a criminal (as opposed to a political) prisoner, he was of course liberated many months before the rest of us. A couple of years afterwards, as I walked down the street in Budapest one day,

someone suddenly grabbed my wrist from behind, and I
turned to find Talian kneeling in a puddle, kissing my hand,
and sobbing repeatedly: "Forgive me! Forgive me!" It was
such a lunatic, Dostoyevskian scene that until today I had all
but forgotten it.

*   *   *

In the meantime, here I am in this posh little dacha, well fed,
warm, in a silk-screen landscape of green on silver—and my
mind, today, has been an utter blank. But if the *RCMP* (or
whoever) should suddenly burst in, rifle my papers, rip
open the mattress, throw books off the shelves, slap me
around, shove me into a car, and remove me to the nearest
dungeon, then, once the initial shock wore off, I would
huddle in the corner between the plank bed and the drain
in the cement floor and begin muttering to myself the
opening lines of the poem that would, inevitably, have
occurred to me.

So it was over three decades ago when, as a guest of the
Hungarian Secret Police, I found my muse (as our grand-
fathers called her) constantly at my side. During one nine-
month period of blessedly solitary confinement, as I ex-
tracted by hand the fragments of broken teeth, she never
shut up. Starved and frozen, I huddled on the stone floor
making a sort of tent of my verminous coat, breathing into a
sleeve to warm my body, and made poems all day long.
They came, some days, almost faster than one could com-
mit them to memory.

The point, if there is one, is that art, the chief task of
which is to enhance life by giving one a passion for it, is
produced at least as often in death-in-life circumstances as
in ideal ones. We are a strange and perverse species.

*   *   *

There has been a panel discussion on the radio about the
fact that the world's population will reach five thousand
million this summer. There is to be a *celebration* of the

event at the United Nations, if anyone can believe it. During the programme an American academic mentioned in mournful tones that the birthrate of the Western world (by which of course he meant "white") is, however, declining. Each year "we" become a smaller fraction of the teeming whole.

This, in the face of a looming disaster nobody seems to believe in, was a classic example in the category of Beside the Point. Listening to the man I could only think: "Gee, that's too bad."

*   *   *

Apropos overpopulation, in one of his letters from Bombay, E. described the slums and pavements overflowing with human discards, and added grimly: "I've seen the future and it doesn't work."

July 11

Wasted an hour this morning reading Bertrand Russell's *Why I Am Not a Christian*, a rather silly polemic that misses more points than it makes. Russell, like most dogmatic sceptics, is under the impression that the only thing to do with an illusion is to destroy it, an act he finds especially enjoyable if someone else happens to believe in it. That illusions have other uses never so much as occurs to him.

The only thing wrong with illusions is not to recognize them for what they are. The arching trees near the pond and the sunlight streaming though them are not a Gothic vault, nor is there really any Panic demi-god lurking beneath the oak. But who would spoil the morning by dwelling on the fact? That God is love and the sunset red may both be illusions; but only a fool would look in either direction and find, say, hatred in the one and the colour green in the other—or find nothing at all. Occam and Hume were not fools, but they were no wiser than Russell when they

100

pointed to illusion and ordered it to disappear—as if a thing were obliged to exist in order to enrich life. Any child watching Peter Pan knows better, and if a sceptic is really enlightened, he will learn to enjoy some of the things he has so busily and usually needlessly been holding up to ridicule and contempt. Christian truth, debunked, becomes Christian myth, or would become if fanatics of more recent superstitions had not sneeringly deprived it of an existence inconsistently allowed to Greek and Hindu mythology.

There are, so far as one knows, no truths of any sort accessible to the human intellect, only illusions and what we call facts—that two plus two equal four; that down is sometimes up; and that both philosophers and chickens occasionally lay eggs.

*   *   *

July 12

A Vancouver newspaper has taken up the cry that Canada's Armed Forces are in a state of disrepair and inadequate for the defence of the nation.

In military terms Canada is to the United States what Bulgaria is to the Soviet Union. Neither country could conceivably defend itself without the help of its huge neighbour; nor, as an ally, would either be of any crucial benefit in Total War. So what do the advocates of "an adequately armed Canada" really have in mind? The glory of the whole thing, that's what.

A healthy love of one's native or adopted land is sometimes in danger of slipping into nationalism, which differs from patriotism as filial love differs from incest. A nationalist needs a large and visible army marching by (preferably goose-stepping, a movement reeking of sublimated eroticism), followed by tanks and an array of phallic missiles. Like all subliminally erotic thrills, this one is hard for adolescents of all ages to resist.

I have great hopes that the Armed Forces will remain in a

state of moderate disrepair. However American Canada may look outwardly, within it is ticking along nicely even now in what can only be described as British muddle—with a great deal of confusion about the Queen and the flag as symbols of a still rather fluid reality, and with little popular desire to assert itself in the world except as a source of charity and arbitration. Canada surpasses Britain, I think, in what is usually thought of as a pre-eminently British virtue, decency; and no generally decent people feels any truly compelling need to aim the erect phalluses of Apollo, Thor, or Sam at the heavens.

Come World War III, the important question for Canada will in any case not be how many adequately equipped soldiers it has stationed in Norway or Alberta, but how many unradiated young men and women are left alive in, say, Fort Good Hope, Northwest Territories, and what books are in its public library.

*   *   *

On the other hand, considering the apparently inborn homicidal tendencies of mankind, what reason is there to think that after some centuries or millennia the same thing would not happen again?

*   *   *

At first light this morning, I went out for a stroll and visited with a pony and his mother. Standing in the tall wet grass, I leaned against a fence and watched them across the field; then the mare, with the pony keeping pace close beside her, galloped in a beautiful wide arc and came up to me expectantly. But I had nothing to give them, so we just looked at one another awhile until, rather embarrassed, I left.

In the same field, some days ago, a solitary cow was grazing, showing no interest in me whatsoever, though I watched her a long time, thinking about Nadezhda Mandelshtam's dream of acquiring a cow and a peasant hut in rural Russia, of hiding out in the provinces and so perhaps escaping the fate that destroyed her husband. Of course she never got together enough money for a cow, let alone a hut, and in *Hope Against Hope* she dreamed: "Perhaps in capitalist countries there might be people eccentric enough to give an exiled poet the money to buy himself a peasant hut and a cow, but there could be no question of it here."

It is a pleasant fantasy, and as the Mandelshtams never went into exile in the West they were spared that particular disillusion at least.

*   *   *

I had thought once that by turning my finches loose in a room I was making them free and secure at the same time, and found it ridiculous that, after each nibble of food, they would stand on tiptoe and look around for enemies. Then I remembered how in the Japanese, sniper-infested jungles of New Guinea we used to eat much the same way. And later, in Recsk, we drank our watery soup with an eye permanently watching for a guard. One can't turn tropical finches out-of-doors in this country, but the only alternative, it seems, is to be regarded by them as the commandant of an aviary Buchenwald.

*   *   *

The phrase "God created man in His own image" does not make one particularly eager to meet Him.

July 13

Halfway to the pond early this evening the far sightedness of old age (you can't see to shave, but distance is no problem) presented me for a moment with a group of shrews creeping along like elf-monks on their way to prayer: an inevitable fantasy-illusion at the spot in the path, where a huge cedar with spiral-fluting winds its way upwards and expands, as in King's College Chapel, into a heaven of fan-vaulting and tracery. Beyond the pond the sun settled into the tree tops, and one felt the furry silence like ear muffs. At this spot I am reminded daily of something equally true of Toronto, though it would take a strenuous leap of the imagination to realize it there: this land is unhaunted. When darkness falls, no ghosts emerge—at least none perceptible to my non-aboriginal senses—to make the short hairs stand and the pulse quicken.

For a European it is an odd, even disconcerting thing to be in a landscape that is just that, landscape. Almost every inch of *his* native region, on the other hand, has at one time or another been drenched in human blood, heard the shout of victory or the moan of defeat, and been filled to a depth of at least six feet with the detritus of past generations, with the whole business recorded, usually in Latin, in the local archives. *Here* everyone walks like Adam in Eden, and the European exile has the additional disorientation of feeling like Ruth amid the alien corn.

Stroll a few hours in almost any direction in this huge country and the chances are that you will have stepped on at least one patch of earth heretofore untrodden by human foot. And this is perhaps the obvious explanation for the constant experimentation and tentativeness in a lot of Canadian writing (as opposed to Canadian painting): there is a distinct limit to what can be said about primaeval nature. No wonder so many Canadian poets rush to the city to congregate in pubs and coffeehouses. Travel (which is going where others have been) has inspired quite a lot of good poetry; exploration very little; downright botany, as far as I know, none at all.

Most poetry, like civilization itself, is in some degree the vicarious use of other people's lives. The philistine is apt to think of nature as a source of "artistic inspiration"; in fact, except for a few like Wordsworth, it is for artists what it is for most other people: where you go to get away from it all.

*   *   *

104

A young American poet has sent me a volume of his work with a flattering dedication and a request that I give him my criticism. Why, I ask, don't they leave criticism to the critics? The answer is probably that few critics bother reviewing poetry nowadays because few people in the English-speaking world read the stuff. Less than three percent of the population, I am told, read books. The number reading poetry must be a tiny fraction of one percent, and if this is so it is, I suspect, because most of what is written nowadays is cryptic, clever-clever, flat and, dear God, boring. Boredom is death to any art, and modern poetry has committed suicide with it.

The truth seems to be that a not quite first-rate poem, couched in some form the ear can recognize, final syllables bejewelled with the diamonds of rhyme or at least the rhinestones of assonance, still stands a better chance of being accorded a hearing than does the same poem stripped of its traditional garments and left begging on one's doorstep in the nasal whine of postmodernism.

If it is really true that the old forms, like Nietzsche's God, are dead and have long since begun to stink in the nostrils of the young, then let the young find new forms. That is precisely what they have done, however primitively, in their music, and they've done it instinctively. Therein lies the problem. In its effect, music is the least intellectual of the arts. Literature, the production or even the enjoyment of which requires some degree of intellectual effort, cannot be made instinctively. In music a young man or woman with passions to express (and which of them has not?) will, given a modicum of talent, automatically slip into some form or other (*i.e.*, a recognizable measure, key, harmonic patterns, etc.). But let them turn to poetry and, as language has to strive and contrive to reach the same end, they fall on their faces.

I don't know what to write to the young man in Chicago. His poems are full of interesting images and ideas: they're like shorthand notes for poems waiting to be written, melodies picked out on the keyboard with one finger.

*   *   *

Mrs. McN. frowns with disapproval when, every three or four days, I buy a packet of cigarettes from her. Does she think it's going to stunt my growth? Smoking is admittedly a foolish habit, and one notes with approval that it is slowly dying out, though more quickly than elsewhere in North America, where illusions about the essential nature of life are long-lived, and where death holds more terrors than it does for older and more cynical races such as the chain-smoking Chinese.

There is in North America a certain unreflective attitude towards life (the soil in which trendiness flourishes) that permits people to indulge in the destruction of their own environment while singling out, without the slightest sense of irony, things like tobacco for stern disapproval. When it comes to the quality of life, not to mention longevity, I am not at all certain that cigarettes are deadlier on the whole than cars.

No doubt the world will one day be the better for the disappearance of tobacco, but in the meantime it might be well for those fanatically against it to remember that the worst that can be said of it is that it is addictive, messy, enjoyable, and very hazardous, *i.e.*, much like life itself. Not that this will stop them. The censuring of vices that one does not happen to share has long been, like chess and democracy, a Mecca for little minds.

July 14

Crawling beneath the writing desk to retrieve a dropped cigarette, I discovered several feet of books that had escaped my notice, most notably the journal of Stephen MacKenna, an Irish newspaperman who gave up his profession, income, and health to spend the rest of his life translating the neo-Platonist philosopher Plotinus. Plotinus no longer interests me, not even in MacKenna's glorious translation, but thumbing through the journal I once again came across the irritable footnote in which he said that nothing better illustrated the inveterate stupidity of mankind than its choice of Christianity over neo-Platonism.

There was a time in my dreamy youth when I agreed with that, but no more. A belief in the divine, whether conceived in the fashion of the Greeks or that of the Hebrews, does not now strike me as stupid—although its frequent result, a glazed-eyed staring into never-never land, and the assumption of the possession of Truth, does. Far more congenial to my earth-bound imagination is the doctrine of Epicurus of Samos, who believed in the existence of the gods without making much fuss about it. It seemed to Epicurus that, in the absence of any evidence to the contrary, they did not interfere in human affairs.

Thinking about MacKenna, Epicurus, and all that, I walked this afternoon beyond the pond where, in a little glade that is obviously a gathering place for elves and trolls on moonlit nights, there stands a large boulder, one surface of which is smooth and fairly invites an inscription. Ever since youth I have had a sort of mad hankering, whenever confronted with such a *saxum immortale*, to acquire a hammer and chisel and carve for all posterity my very best lines (whatever they may be!)—an ambition likely to be fulfilled, if at all, only on a tombstone one day.

Today that rock put me in mind of a man who had a nobler, less egotistical ambition. His name was Diogenes and he was a businessman in the town of Oenoanda in Asia Minor. In old age, with death approaching, Diogenes used his wealth to erect a huge stone wall many yards long upon which he had inscribed the principal tenets of the philosophy that had given him happiness throughout his life, that of Epicurus. History records few acts more agreeable than this one of a man who, without intending to, earned immortality by it. The simple, meditative, friendly, ascetic, altruistic, and altogether disciplined hedonism of Epicurus still seems to me the instinctive philosophy of most happy people, and (to paraphrase MacKenna) if anything shows the inveterate stupidity of humanity, it is the way it has reviled that philosophy and its founder for over two millennia now, so that "Epicurean" is now the label given to the sort of people who measure happiness by the size of their bank accounts and the quality and frequency of their orgasms.

Leaning against the black, moss-covered boulder, I dropped my little ambition for granite-inscribed immortality. Let it stay covered with moss and lichen until someone like Diogenes of Oenoanda comes along again with words as life-affirming as the boulder and the glade themselves. Anything less is just the desecration of a flat surface: subway graffitti, Mount Rushmore.

July 15

Few things are more revealing of people than the books they read and collect, and I have yet to come across a truly bad book in this cottage. Leaving these shelves behind when I return to Toronto is going to be a bit painful, for Toronto is anything but a book-lover's paradise. Florence, a quarter of its size, has more and better bookshops, and almost any comparable American city has a better public library system.

Though grateful for its existence, I must admit that the public library of Metropolitan Toronto is pretty inadequate. Its more than thirty branches are not very well stocked and the Central Reference Library has so few books in its open stacks (and not all that many in the closed ones) that it looks more like a book-exhibition than a library: miles of carpeting, potted plants and expensive architecture and, here and there, a few books. For someone who reads in order to write, and writes in order to live, it's all fairly discouraging. If the governments concerned had put *half* the astronomical amounts of money spent on the new Toronto Public Library and the Robarts Library of the University of Toronto

into the augmentation of their collections, Toronto would
have two of North America's better libraries. As it is, one
looks in vain most of the time for even slightly out-of-the-
way books, sometimes even for standard texts.

*   *   *

By accident I discovered that the kitchen radio has a short-
wave band. Perhaps the damp atmosphere, or the prox-
imity to the sea, helps reception, for when I switched it on
this evening Radio Tirana (Albania) came booming out at
me. The Albanians broadcast with so much power that one
imagines all the lights in the country dimming when they
go on the air. It is strange, sitting in a British Columbia
kitchen, listening to that voice from the past, a Stalinist
announcer going on and on (in English, no less) with forced,
fruity enthusiasm about over-fulfilled milk quotas, the demands of the working masses, the whole nauseating Newspeak vocabulary about fighting for peace, dollar-leashed
puppets of capitalism, and all the rest of it. (Fighting for
peace, as someone once said, is like fucking for chastity.) It's
astonishing how exactly you can gauge the quality of life in
a country by its radio programmes. Albania must be
positively Orwellian, worse even than Hungary before the
Greatest Friend of the Working Masses finally suffered a
cerebral hemorrhage in the Kremlin and slipped off to hell
after what I hope was a very slow death.

*   *   *

Apropos Stalin, I remember my friend, Stephen Dobos,
telling me about the Hungarian delegation's visit to him
after the war. Steve went as secretary to the President of the
Republic. The Hungarians were lined up on the polished
floors of the huge Vladimir Hall in the Kremlin and waited,
sweating with nervousness, until at last Stalin entered followed by Molotov and the rest of his entourage. Beside
Stalin an aide stood whispering the names and functions of
each of the Hungarians. When the Father of Progressive

Mankind got to Steve, he looked impressed: "What? Only twenty-two years old and already secretary to the President of the Republic? You'll go high, young man, *very high!*" As he said this, Stalin sketched an imaginary noose around his own neck and, raising his arm, pretended to hang himself. Then he laughed softly and move on to the next man—and potential victim.

*   *   *

And now to bed, reflecting, as I sometimes do, on the lovely and unexpected words of the 12th century scholar Bernard of Chartres: "A humble mind, a love of learning, a quiet life, a silent searching, poverty and exile: for many these are the keys to happiness."

July 16

Still unable to write with any enthusiasm. Browsing through books is one thing, but if you become engrossed in a good novel, as I did the other night, you're ruined for the time being: It either drives off incipient inspiration or, worse, leaves you unconsciously imitating its own style.

Giving it up again last night, I turned in early and attempted to defeat insomnia by the only two methods I know. The first is to lie there staring straight ahead through closed eyelids. The theory is that the eyes will become heavy and lower themselves as in sleep. It never works, but feels as if it ought to. Neither does the second method, learned from my old friend Alexander Lenard; but it at least has the advantage of being mildly entertaining.

Lenard had an occasional preoccupation with what he called the "lineage of handshakes" *i.e.*, to discover how many handshakes removed he was from various interesting, or at least famous, people. During the war, for instance, he met the German humanist Hans Carossa in Rome. Carossa had once shaken the hand of the historian Curtius, who in turn had shaken the hand of the dying Heinrich Heine in Paris. Heine had once met Goethe. Thus Lenard (whom I can visualize lying awake in his house in the Brazilian rainforest as I've been doing here) was only three handclasps removed from the Sage of Weimar.

At two or three in the morning, in the faintly ominous silence that pervades houses between midnight and dawn, I lay there trying to work out an even closer relationship with Goethe, but could not. On the other hand, by virtue of having shaken the hands of Franklin Delano Roosevelt, Thomas Mann, and Rustem Vámbéry, I found myself only once removed from a glittering array of people ranging from Vaslav Nijinsky to Queen Victoria. Before dawn broke and I finally drifted off to sleep, I had worked out a probable sixth-degree removal from Mozart (through Hayden, five princes Esterházy, and Count Michael Károlyi). A pointless game, perhaps, but it does make one feel oddly close in time to some of those one most admires (not to mention a few one loathes).

*   *   *

Better watch out for this sort of thing. The desk-bound creator is often prone to little obsessions. Dr. Johnson used, I think, to be a compulsive lamp-post counter; Anton Bruckner would stand freezing in the snow trying to count the bare branches of trees; Daniel Heinsius would sometimes greet the dawn bleary-eyed, having spent the night mentally listing anagrams on the names of Roman emperors.

*   *   *

The subject of insomnia has reminded me for the first time in years of an old acquaintance of mine, a Jewish journalist named Paul Királyhegyi who, in 1951, was confused by the Secret Police with Count Királyhegyi and exiled from Budapest to the countryside during the period when the aristocrats of Hungary were condemned to live in cowsheds and the like. (No longer: Snobbery has won out over socialism, and the aristocrats of Hungary, if not exactly rolling in clover, suffer no social handicaps nowadays, to say the least.)

Királyhegyi ended up in a pigsty, and when he managed to write to us in Budapest, he complained that the noise of the pigs and the revels of the peasants were depriving him of sleep to the point he felt he was going mad. Could we, he asked, send him some sleeping pills? My wife Zsuzsa immediately took up a collection of barbiturates—sleeping powder was for some reason abundant during those years of chronic shortages—and we sent Királyhegyi a large parcel of the stuff. Some weeks later we received another note, this one ecstatic. "It's heaven," he wrote. "I've been putting the powder in the water hole, and neither the peasants nor the pigs get up until noon."

*   *   *

There's been a big "peace conference" in Moscow and everyone who's anyone is flocking to it. If the Americans tried to hold the same sort of thing people would sneer, as the Americans are of course "war mongers." The Canadian delegates would do well to remember that if the Soviet Union were their neighbour to the south, they would no longer have to cross a border to get to its peace conferences. There wouldn't be one anymore.

July 17

Early this afternoon work actually began to *go*. Shoving everything off the kitchen table (for some reason most writers I know, like myself, head for the kitchen table when inspiration arrives unexpectedly), I hastily scribbled the lines as they began pouring in. Then there was a knock on the door. The nice people from the Hobbit-house had dropped in for tea with their little daughter.

They really are charming kids, but, like most of the young, unable to imagine that they are not always and everywhere welcome. Resigned to my fate, I poured them tea and chatted until around dinnertime, when they left. I am still always amazed at the way so many people assume that a writer's time is always free. People who would not dream of bursting in upon a dentist in the act of earning his living will cheerfully interrupt a writer as if doing him a great favour. This ought to be a salutary reminder of the world's actual priorities; but it just leaves me tired, irritable and, of course, drained of inspiration.

E., when writing his Latin poems, unplugs the telephone, refuses to answer the door, and once was witnessed working right through a highrise fire alarm. I suggested that I probably ought to imitate him, but he replied: "You can't. A lot of people adore you because you give them the impression that they're more important to you than your work. You have a front to keep up."

We never know ourselves as well as others do.

*   *   *

"Why does many a man write? Because he does not possess enough character not to write."

— *Karl Kraus*

*   *   *

A letter from E. yesterday, postmarked Mussoorie, U.P.:

Events enroute from New Delhi to Mussoorie included a rest stop at a "jungle park" where, as I followed a trail to the privy, a long (very long) snake raced across the path just ahead of me. When the bus pulled into Dehra Doon, a ragged woman stood below my window and held a bag up for my inspection; it contained a snake which she held loosely (too loosely) up to me until I gave her a rupee to put it away. I took a taxi from there up the breath-taking road to Mussoorie, 7000 feet above. About a mile before the town a bus rounded the corner on the right (*i.e.*, wrong) side of the road. Both vehicles braked, skidded, collided gently; and the bus, unable to stop completely, pushed the taxi back in a series or remarkable hops until we backed into a milestone at the edge. Getting out I saw that the drop we had so narrowly avoided was perhaps 2000 feet. A great altercation ensued, in the midst of which, bored, I paid the driver and walked the rest of the way to town through the clouds. The scenery was unimaginably beautiful, all peaks, jungle-covered cliffs and mist.

I checked in at Hackmann's Hotel and went strolling down the Mall for lunch. In front of the post office a crowd watched as a small but ferocious dog cornered a little girl, who was too terrified even to scream. As nobody seemed inclined to do anything about it, I kick-lifted the dog and sent it flying into a stone wall. It backed off then, still snarling. "You want to watch out," a middle-aged onlooker reproved me in superior tones, "that dog is certainly rabid." I toyed with the idea of kick-lifting him into the wall, but rejected it.

India is an emotional roller-coaster: one minute it fills you with affection and the next it plunges you into contempt, even fury.

My final encounter for the day with an animal was a large rat running around the room before I went to bed, with me chasing it with an umbrella. Mr. Fodor, a fan of yours I believe, describes Hackmann's in his guide book as "first-class superior." Had Mr. Fodor been there I would have chased *him* with my umbrella.

Today was better. I took my portable cassette player and hiked out of town, climbed the highest hill hereabouts, and was rewarded with a view extending almost from Nepal to Pakistan, with numerous peaks along the Tibetan border in between, most of them over 20,000 feet. It is mouth-openingly spectacular. The sun glints blindingly off those ice-bound mountains many miles away, and as one sits there it disappears intermittently as monsoon-clouds scud up and wrap one in candy floss.

I played the Bach I had brought along, Schönberg's arrangement of *Schmücke dich, o liebe Seele*. Planned aesthetic experiences tend not to come off, but this one did. The greatest music in the world soaring out in the silence of the greatest landscape in the world, it filled me with wonder and a shuddering joy at being *alive*.

It is rather cold at this height when the sun disappears, so I bought a woollen dressing gown from a Tibetan merchant for one-hundred rupees (a coat was too expensive) and now present a bizarre figure, roaming the hills in my dressing gown with an umbrella in one hand and a Hindi grammar in the other. This being an old, ragtag and subtly sophisticated civilization, my eccentric appearance warrants not the slightest glance from anyone. I look, and feel, like Kipling's Hurree Babu.

July 18

More mist and light rain here too. I splashed out to the mailbox by the road to find that Jacqueline had forwarded an invitation to join a health club ("for those on their way to the top") and the following mystifying but entertaining piece of invective:

Sir:

A month ago I sent you a letter about the opprobrious treatment I got from your representatives while trying to find out about items stolen from my bags at O'Hare Airport. You have not answered.

To be fair, I suppose if I were overpaid managerial deadwood in a company with a public relations policy modelled on Genghis Khan's, I too would cringe in anonymous irresponsibility behind a phalanx of mindless representatives who produce, with physiological regularity, such utterances as "There's nothing we can do."

The next time someone asks me to "Give the United Way" I will be able to reply that I already have.

(Signed) J. L. Spellman"

I was wondering who Mr. Spellman was and which of us was mad when it occurred to me to look at the envelope and realize that the letter was a copy sent to E. by his old army buddy, Lucian, in Arizona.

I myself have been comparatively lucky in the matter of dealing with airlines. Air France once temporarily sent all my luggage to Teheran instead of Tangier; and on another occasion when I arrived late at Orly a helpful official hustled me at breakneck speed onto a plane bound, as it turned out, for Madrid, not Casablanca. Profuse apologies awaited me at the other end, as did a free hotel room, and I spent a delightful morning looking at Hieronymous Bosch in the Prado before hopping Royal Air Maroc (free) to Casablanca.

*   *   *

Twice this afternoon I opened my Hungarian-English dictionary, a tome of some thousands of pages, to exactly the page containing the word I was looking for. Is this one of the things Koestler was talking about in his *Roots of Coincidence*, or is it a sign of advanced pedantry, a sort of *dernier cri* in philological refinement?

*   *   *

A long-delayed letter from Zagreb, telling me the latest story. There is always a shortage of something or other in the East Block, and in Yugoslavia at the moment it's apparently coffee that can't be had. It seems Ivan sees Branko walking down the street carrying a bag of coffee. "Where did you get it?" he demands excitedly. "You'll have to go out to the suburbs, to Dugo Selo," says Branko. "What! You mean they've got coffee in the suburbs but not in Zagreb?" exclaims Ivan. "No. You buy it in Zagreb. The queue begins in Dugo Selo."

*   *   *

By putting a volume of the OED on a kitchen chair and standing atop both on tiptoe I can, just, reach the row of books that scrape the ceiling, mostly complete sets of authors few read nowadays. It took me six or seven trips to get all of Anatole France down, and then I wished I had not. Except for *At the Sign of the Reine Pédauque* and *The Garden of Epicurus*, he's pretty heavy going now, though I loved him in my youth. It's hard to imagine now what a furor his Epicureanism and gentle eroticism aroused in the 1920s, with bishops howling imprecations from their pulpits. The pages of the present set (published in 1912 by John Lane Company, with translations by Mrs. Wilfrid Jackson) crumble as I turn them. Until now I had thought that "self-destructing" paper was not invented until recently.

July 19

At the risk of being the last person in the world to hear about World War III or the Second Coming, I have decided to read no more newspapers for the time being and to leave the radio switched off. It is not so much the endless round of human violence and villainy that leaves me tired and dispirited (that has been with us since the beginning) but the insistent, whining *demand* for this and that coming from every conceivable quarter. Subway conductors in Paris, postmen in Toronto, B.C. longshoremen, anyone with less than fifty times the income of the average Peruvian farmer or Bangkok pedicab driver is howling for a bigger piece of the pie; every socially oppressed, despised, or merely envious group is demanding what it assumes to be justice.

Somehow along the road from the revolutionary howl of 1848 to the British welfare state, something was lost, *viz.*, the knowledge that all real progress in human affairs is the result of striving, not demanding. What happened was Karl Marx, who announced with undeniable plausibility that those who produce have a right to the fruits of that production; and, with less plausibility, that the way to realize that right is to demand it. The other thing that happened was fascism, the essential message of which is: "We (name of group) have special rights, which we demand!"

The obvious reply—a truism I am boringly reminded of every time I hear the news—is this: Indeed we do have rights, but to demand them, instead of striving for them, is intrinsically violent. And (one may well ask at this point) so what? Just this: What is always demanded is justice. We do indeed have a right to justice, and accordingly a duty to do it. Each of us requires a measure of patience, forbearance, and good-will from his fellow man, and therefore each of us owes it in return. In some contexts this is called justice; in others it is called charity. However paradoxical it may sound, they are, ultimately, the same thing and violence obliterates them both. Justice is never, despite all appearances to the contrary, the product of violence. It follows that it is not to be had on demand.

*   *   *

E. writes from the Himalayas that a shopkeeper in the hill town of Mussoorie has a tiny Lhasa Apso puppy in an open drawer behind the counter. But for the impossibility of bringing it all the way to Canada (not to mention keeping it in my tiny apartment), he would have bought it for me. I have always missed my Moroccan dog, Matapan.

Moroccans tend to be cruel to animals, especially dogs (whom the Prophet despised), and once during the war when I was sitting in a Tangier coffeehouse a badly beaten dog crawled along the wall under the couches until she reached me, and there she huddled, trembling, with her nose against my ankle. The waiter chased her out, and when I followed a moment later she was waiting for me hopefully in the street. She bowed her head eagerly when I took off my belt to use as a leash, and when we got home and I pointed to the little rug beside my bed, she lay down at once and went to sleep.

When morning came I inspected her: she was extremely dirty and had been injured by blows, with her nose split and still bloody, but she was beautiful for all that. I gave her some milk and was about to wash her when suddenly she jumped out of the window and ran off. A few minutes later she reappeared from the direction of the playground of the Spanish girls' school and gently laid a sandwich in my hand with an air of triumph.

A few days later, when she was clean and already in much better health, an Arab approached us in the street and demanded her back. The dog was in the meantime trying to hide behind me. "She's mine now," I said. The Arab demanded a hundred *dirhams* for her. "Not one *centime*," I replied. He kept lowering the price until finally, exasperated, I suggested we let the *Kadi* decide.

We found the judge, a bearded old gentleman in a turban, sitting in his courtyard, and explained the facts to him. He took ten *dirhams* from each of us, then said: "I'll hold the dog. You walk twenty paces to the right, and you, Nazarene, twenty to the left." We obeyed and then he let the dog loose to choose her own master.

After becoming the legal owner of Matapan, I named her in honour of a naval battle, for on the day she first found me in the café the Axis agents (who were numerous in Tangier) were going around with gloomy looks on their faces: The British had destroyed the Italian fleet off Cape Matapan in Greece.

*   *   *

A memory illustrating the incredibly and incurably petit

bourgeois nature of Budapest society. There were during my childhood large numbers of beggars in the city, many of them war amputees who paddled along on wheeled platforms or in little carts. Among these, I noticed, only those were regularly given alms who had on shirt-fronts, vests, and neckties. It did not matter how dirty or ragged: The fact that they wore them put their owners among the "deserving poor." At least I assume this was the rationale; I may be wrong. Right-wing Hungarian exiles, including not a few former Nazis, frequently accuse me of not really understanding the folkways of traditional Hungarian society, an accusation to which I happily plead guilty.

*   *   *

Has anyone ever noticed how American the Emperor Augustus looks in all the many surviving statues? By the time he was twenty that ruthless youth had experienced more and bloodier adventures than the next ten men put together, but none of it shows in his smooth, rather bland and Californian features.

American faces have often astonished me in the same way: open, pleasant, and utterly unrevealing of whatever character may lurk beneath. Referring to President Eisenhower, someone or other once remarked how many elderly American look like aged babies. They've had two centuries of history now, but the first lines have yet to appear in the national face.

July 20

Dr. Ödön Berzsenyi, who died several years ago in Toronto, was a perfect example of a gentleman of the old school and much admired by all his fellow inmates in the concentration camp at Recsk.

After a day spent cutting down trees or splitting rocks, trembling with cold and exhaustion, almost hallucinating with hunger, we used to try after dark to keep our spirits up and our minds alive by lecturing quietly to one another, each talking about the subject he knew best. As we were Hungarians, poetry, music, and history were our chief sustenance, but from time to time philosophy would be discussed.

On one of these occasions, when we were trying to make some sort of sense of our century and our own fates, Berzsenyi, who was not generally given to philosophizing, suddenly insisted in tones that brooked no opposition: "Ethics and aesthetics are the same thing." None of us could make much of that, but the unexpected, not to say paradoxical, proposition remained firmly in mind, and one day several years later in London, I came across the same flat assertion in the *Tractatus* of Ludwig Wittgenstein. It remained baffling.

The other day the truth of the matter was at last spelled out for me by a passage in Santayana's *The Sense of Beauty*:

> Not only are the various satisfactions which morals are meant to secure aesthetic in the last analysis, but when the conscience is formed, and right principles acquire an immediate authority, our attitude to these principles becomes aesthetic also. Honour, truthfulness and cleanliness are obvious examples. When the absence of these virtues causes an instinctive disgust, as it does in well-bred people, the reaction is essentially aesthetic...It is *kalokagathia*, the aesthetic demand for the morally good, and perhaps the finest flower of human nature.

July 22

I dreamed last night that an archeologist had unearthed the lost chapters of Petronius' masterpiece the *Satyricon*. I grabbed it from him and would not give it back, and when I awoke at dawn his desperate pleas were still ringing in my ears: *"Sie müssen es mir geben! Sie müssen!"* But I wouldn't do it.

*   *   *

At the tomb of Heinrich Heine in Montmartre there is a little box so that visitors can drop in their *cartes de visite*, as the poet wished. I read today, and was strangely touched by the account, that many German soldiers during the war defied the anti-Semitism of their leaders and, having no cards, left flowers there. I hope that Heine, from wherever supremely gifted poets go when they die, was watching.

After their most recent war, in which so many I loved were butchered by them, or gassed in Auschwitz, or, like my sister, a physician, were shot and thrown into the Danube by their Hungarian followers, my mind tends to go numb when confronted with the fact of Germany. Descriptions of humanity or kindness on the part of Germans move me now more than similar accounts of Americans or Finns would. The unexpected always touches us more strongly.

July 24

I had got about a hundred yards down the road in the direction of the store this morning when a police car slowed down and "pulled me over," as they say, though of course I was on foot. Permanently and hopelessly East European, my first reaction was a little twinge of fear because I wasn't carrying my passport. But a smiling face leaned out the window, wished me good morning, and asked: "You the poet?" I confessed immediately, and the boy (all policemen look about sixteen to me nowadays) offered me a ride, which I declined, perhaps a little too effusively. The truth is, I'm allergic to police cars, even Canadian ones

I've often wondered just what one would do if a policeman in this country demanded one's "papers," since nowhere in the English-speaking world (with the not unexpected exception of South Africa) is one required as far as I know to have any. Unlike police states such as Hungary and the Soviet Union, or semi-police states such as France, countries like England, Canada, and the United States do not require their citizens to carry "internal passports" or any of those other documents that make it easy for some governments to locate citizens when they feel like arresting and torturing them. This is not generally appreciated for what it is, a singular blessing. No one who has not grown up in a country where they open a police file on you the day you're born can possible understand the slight distaste I even now feel towards such benign, not to say beneficent, documents as my social insurance and senior citizen's cards.

I remember hearing on the radio one day in the early '70s that the Prime Minister, Pierre Trudeau, had suggested in Parliament that Canadians be given European-style identity cards. The idea was rejected contemptuously by all three parties, but I remember thinking at the time that it was not the sort of thing that would have occurred to an Anglo-Saxon liberal, or for that matter to anyone who had any very exact notion as to what liberalism was all about.

The truth is, I always rather liked Pierre Trudeau. He was obviously a gentleman: one noted with satisfaction how he slapped the face of a heckler who was insolent on the subject of his wife; also how at the convention that first nominated him he, almost alone in the auditorium, sat through the speeches of lame-duck candidates with eccentric doctrines and no chances of winning. And then there was his faultless bilingual oratory, so intelligent and persuasive that one was very often tempted to believe him even if he *was* a politician. (It was rather like Charles de Gaulle pretending to be Edmund Burke: at once entertaining and impressive; and, as subsequent history has shown, a hard act to follow.) But when he came up with the bright idea of identity cards, I, along with untold numbers of other fugitives from the Land of the Midnight Arrest, felt a chill as the words registered, and never voted Liberal again in a federal election.

July 28

When the Soviet Army conquered, occupied, and then began ruling the various nations of Eastern Europe at the end of World War II, the first emotions they induced in the population (who, after the Nazis, naïvely thought they had seen everything), were horror and terror in the face of mass rape, indiscriminate execution, and a level of barbarism so profound that human communication often seemed impossible. Once this first stage was over, a new emotion came in its wake: a savagely amused contempt for their pretension of being a "superior culture." By now, four decades later, there is scarcely an East European working in any profession who has not at one time or another been confronted by some clown imported from Elektrogorsk or Yeseningrad come to "teach" East Germans how to make generators, or Hungarians how to write poetry.

To an East European the depressing thing about so many Russian dissidents in recent years is the way they have accepted this more than dubious superiority as a fact. Aleksandr Solzhenitsyn takes for granted in a way that sounds slightly unhinged by now that Mother Russia has a spiritual mission in the world; and Vladimir Bukovsky, also a man of proven personal courage (and even greater journalistic ability), has recently graduated from autobiography to the fine old Soviet art of laying down the law for us on any number of subjects—European subjects which Europeans had thought largely their own affair.

It is even more depressing that the West continues to swallow this rubbish. Russian culture is, or once was, one of the world's greatest, but after three-quarters of a century of Tartar Socialism, it lives largely in memory. Nadezhda Man-

delshtam, among others, has demonstrated that it died of a
bullet in the neck in the 1930s, if not earlier.

July 29

On a branch before the house this morning sat the most
beautiful bird I have ever seen in Canada, not counting my
own tropical finches, and I have no idea what it was. Something between a giant budgie and a small parrot. Whatever
it is, it knows it is beautiful, for as I watched it raised its large
beak haughtily—like a woman who knows she is being
observed—and then hid its face coyly in the feather boa of a
wing.

*   *   *

Koestler has been on my mind these past few days, after I
thumbed yet again through his masterpiece, *Darkness at
Noon*. He was a good, if temperamental, friend when my
wife and I moved to England in 1957, inviting us often, but
ordering us out of his house in Kent one winter night after
an argument at the dinner table. Then, as we struggled
through the snow, he overtook us in his car to apologize
and bring us back. He was very Hungarian.

I phoned him one morning in 1958 to tell him that two
Hungarian writers had just been sentenced to death for
having sided with the Revolution two years earlier. He
phoned Bertrand Russell, then asked me to accompany
Paul Ignotus to Oxford the same morning, which I did. We
presented ourselves before Russell, who was less than
thrilled about "protesting yet again," but who nevertheless
agreed to do so. "But what shall I do?" We gave him
Koestler's message: Wire the Hungarian premier, Janos Ka-
dar, and say, "I, Bertrand Russell, protest against the death
sentences of Gali and Obersovsky and request clemency. If
this is not given, I shall leave the Peace Movement and
inform Premier Khrushchev of the reason."

Russell was clearly amused at the idea and phoned in the telegram on the spot. Ignotus and I returned to London where, *that same evening*, we heard Radio Budapest announce that clemency had been granted both men.

My only question concerning Arthur was always how a man with a brain like that had ever become a Marxist in his youth.

July 30

A postcard from Rajasthan with these neo-Mediaeval Latin lines:

> Miror quare paupertatem,
> dulcem mihi libertatem,
> omnes fere timeant:
>
> sinit illa me vagari
> hominesque contemplari,
> ut non memet videant.

Which means something like: "I wonder why it is that nearly all fear poverty. It gives me liberty to roam the world observing all, while none so much as look at me."

E. likes the idea of doing things that have probably never been done before, like playing Schönberg for the gods of Gangotri. I strongly suspect that these are the first (and last) lines of Goliardic verse ever "composed while sitting amongst inquisitive monkeys in a Jaipur park."

July 31

Tempus est abire. Time to go home. Mrs. McN's son came by to help me put the cottage in order, a task that took us (mostly him) all afternoon and was worth more than the money he reluctantly accepted. Anatole France is back on the top shelf, the bathroom is clean, likewise the kitchen. The heap of linen (which I washed by stacking it in the bathtub and trampling it like an Italian vintner) is stored away as dry as anything ever gets on Vancouver Island, and my more unsightly contributions to the compost heap have been covered with earth. Between now and 10:00 a.m. tomorrow, I must mend my ways and wash each cup and spoon after use.

I took a last walk to the pond this afternoon to say goodbye to the trees, the moss, and the hidden animals. I'm going to miss all this back in my Toronto apartment, where nature is represented by two struggling Benjamina trees and the tiny finches who inhabit them when not perching on the shower rod in the bathroom or, like their master, sometimes staring disconsolately out the window at the endless acres of windswept concrete.

On the other hand, Jacqueline will be waiting with a pot of Nuwara Eliya tea, real croissants from Charles Street, and conversation. And, in a few days, E. will be home with new books from India, a bag of "wonderful pebbles hand-polished by Tibetans in Garhwal," and lots of stories and Latin poems.

These two months have been a splendid gift, a time of silence in which to read, to write, to wander the edge of the forest and, in the depth of night, the heart of my own mental universe. But then the nine hundred and eighteen months before them were also a gift; and so, whatever happens, will be the ones remaining.

Books in English by George Faludy

My Happy Days in Hell

Translated by Kathleen Szasz
London: André Deutsch, 1962
Toronto: William Collins, 1985

City of Splintered Gods

Translated by Flora Papastavrou
London: Eyre and Spottiswoode, 1966
New York: William Morrow, 1966

Erasmus of Rotterdam

Translated by Eric Johnson
London: Eyre and Spottiswoode, 1970
New York: Stein and Day, 1970

East and West: Selected Poems

Edited by John Robert Colombo
Toronto: Hounslow Press, 1978

Learn This Poem of Mine by Heart

Edited by John Robert Colombo
Toronto: Hounslow Press, 1983

Twelve Sonnets

Translated by Robin Skelton
Victoria: Pharos Press, 1983

George Faludy: Selected Poems 1933-80

Edited and Translated by Robin Skelton
Toronto: McClelland and Stewart, 1985

Corpses, Brats and Cricket Music

Translated by Robin Skelton
Vancouver: William Hoffer, 1987

Printed in Canada